Handpainted Tiles
for your home

 NORTH LIGHT BOOKS
CINCINNATI, OHIO
www.artistsnetwork.com

Diane Trierweiler

Published by North Light Books, an imprint of F+W Publications, Inc., 4700 E. Galbraith Rd., Cincinnati, Ohio, 45236. (800) 289-0963. First edition.

Other fine North Light Books are available from your local bookstore, art supply store or direct from the publisher.

09 08 07 06 05   5 4 3 2 1

Distributed in Canada by Fraser Direct
100 Armstrong Avenue
Georgetown, ON, Canada L7G 5S4
Tel: (905) 877-4411

Distributed in the U.K. and Europe by David & Charles
Brunel House, Newton Abbot, Devon, TQ12 4PU, England
Tel: (+44) 1626 323200, Fax: (+44) 1626 323319
Email: mail@davidandcharles.co.uk

Distributed in Australia by Capricorn Link
P.O. Box 704, Windsor, NSW 2756 Australia
Tel: (02) 4577-3555

Library of Congress Cataloging-in-Publication Data

Trierweiler, Diane
  Handpainted tiles for your home / Diane Trierweiler.--1st ed.
      p. cm.
  Includes index.
  ISBN 1-58180-641-8 (pbk.: alk. paper)
  1. Painting. 2. Tiles. I. Title.
  TT385.T73 2005
  /38.6--dc22
                                                    2005001268

F+W PUBLICATIONS, INC.

- EDITOR **KATHY KIPP**
- PRODUCTION COORDINATOR **KRISTEN HELLER**
- COVER DESIGN **JENNA HABIG**
- INTERIOR DESIGN **LEIGH ANN LENTZ**
- INTERIOR LAYOUT ARTIST **KATHY GARDNER**
- PHOTOGRAPHERS **AL PARRISH**
                          CHRISTINE POLOMSKY
                          TIM GRONDIN
- PHOTO STYLIST **NORA MARTINI**

Metric Conversion Chart

To convert	to	multiply by
Inches	Centimeters	2.54
Centimeters	Inches	0.4
Feet	Centimeters	30.5
Centimeters	Feet	0.03
Yards	Meters	0.9
Meters	Yards	1.1
Sq. Inches	Sq. Centimeters	6.45
Sq. Centimeters	Sq. Inches	0.16
Sq. Feet	Sq. Meters	0.09
Sq. Meters	Sq. Feet	10.8
Sq. Yards	Sq. Meters	0.8
Sq. Meters	Sq. Yards	1.2
Pounds	Kilograms	0.45
Kilograms	Pounds	2.2
Ounces	Grams	28.3
Grams	Ounces	0.035

Dedication

About the Author

Diane Trierweiler was born in Wisconsin but has spent most of her life in Southern California. She began teaching herself to paint in watercolor and oils in 1980. Encouraged by her husband, Diane took a decorative painting class, and after that class said she would some day like to open a decorative painting studio. In 1986 her dream came true, and The Tole Bridge opened its doors in Norco, California. Today, Diane teaches decorative painting and fine art throughout the U.S. and Canada. She works in many different styles, using oils, acrylics and watercolor, and continues her education in fine art and impressionism. She has been a member of the Society of Decorative Painters since 1985. Diane has had four project books published, including *Diane Paints Victorian Treasures*, *Country Lane Flower Shop*, *The Secret Garden* and *Down The Garden Path*, plus two North Light books, *Painting Country Cottages & Gardens* and *Pretty Painted Furniture*. She has produced more than one hundred pattern packets and four videos for the Perfect Palette Studio. Diane has her own line of specialty brushes designed to make it easier for the student to paint landscapes and flowers. Through all of her life's adventures, she still finds teaching the most rewarding. She has a wonderful husband, Gil, and two beautiful grown children, Jami and Jared.

Acknowledgments

Thanks to Kathy Kipp for being my editor on this book and taking wonderful notes that made my job so much easier. I always appreciate your suggestions and ideas. Thanks also to Christine Polomsky, who did the great step-by-step photography for this book and for my first two North Light books as well.

Table of Contents

Getting Started

Painting Supplies

Painting on tiles is easy and fun! For the projects in this book, no firing is required. I used DecoArt Americana acrylic paints from the craft store, and ceramic floor and wall tiles that I bought very inexpensively at my local home improvement center or tile store. If you can't find the size you need, they will cut the tiles for you.

In the photo below are some of the products I use to paint on ceramic floor tiles, glazed wall tiles, and tin ceiling tiles. These are available at your local craft store, or see the Resources section in the back of the book.

- **J.W. etc. UnderCover:** Use this as an undercoating on your tiles or any nonporous surface so the acrylic paint will stick to the surface. It's very durable, has great coverage, and comes in white or black.

- **J.W. etc. Texture Gel Glaze:** Add any color you like to this gel and create your own antiquing medium. It will not dilute the pigment, simply makes it transparent and very movable. I used it over the tissue paper background in project 10 (see page 75).

- **Delta Ceramcoat Two-Step Fine Crackle Finish:** This creates a fine crackle finish on any painted project.

- **Etchall Etching Creme:** Removes small areas of the glazed layer from ceramic wall tiles and gives tooth to glass or mirrors. Your paint won't slip on the surface if you etch it first.

- **Etchall Dip 'n Etch:** This liquid product allows you to completely submerge a tile to remove all the glazing. The liquid can be saved and reused many times.

- **J.W. etc. Gold Metallic Wax:** A very light, beeswax-based metallic. I used this to accent the embossed tin tile wall pocket in project 8 (see page 64).

- **Krylon Matte Finish:** Spray over the two-step crackle finish when dry before applying the white oil paint in project 5 (see page 39).

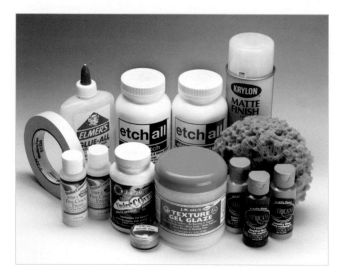

Loew-Cornell 3/4-inch (19mm) Glazing
Loew-Cornell Large Dome
Loew-Cornell Medium Dome
Loew-Cornell Small Dome
Diane T's No. 2 Petal
Diane T's 10/0 Striper
Diane T's No. 4 Petal
Loew-Cornell 10/0 Rake
Loew-Cornell 515-M Berry Maker
Loew-Cornell Medium Berry Maker
Diane T's 3/8-inch (10mm) Angel Wing
Diane T's No. 8 Petal

Brushes

All the projects in this book were painted with Loew-Cornell brushes and my own line, Diane Trierweiler's Signature brushes. Here are some helpful tips on using these brushes.

Below from left to right:

- **Glazing Brush:** for basecoating large areas and for varnishing.

- **Dome Brushes:** for drybrushing and stippling in highlights and shadows.

- **Petal Brushes:** shaped like a filbert but with a tongue-length bristle, for strokework and for blending wet-on-wet.

- **10/0 Striper:** for fine linework such as tendrils or striping.

- **10/0 Rake:** for stippling in very small areas of texture.

- **Berry Maker:** foam applicator, comes in four sizes; for creating berries and berry segments such as raspberries.

- **Angel Wing:** double load with two colors and flip back and forth to create masses of tiny flowers.

- **No. 8 Petal Brush:** used often in this book to create wet-on-wet leaves, etc.

- **Angel Mist:** made of badger hair. Wet the brush, fluff it out on a towel and use to stipple in soft foliage.

- **Angel Hair:** for creating textured backgrounds.

- **Fingertip Brush:** made from golden sable, specially cut bristles make it easy to double load and paint soft clouds or background foliage.

- **1/2-inch (13mm) Petal Brush:** for scumbling backgrounds, painting large stroke flowers and leaves, feathers, and raked effects.

- **Flats:** for basecoating; choose the size appropriate for the design.

- **Angles:** for floating shadows, highlights, and making rose petals.

Diane T's 1/2-inch (13mm) Angel Mist · Diane T's 1/2-inch (13mm) Angel Hair · Diane T's Fingertip Brush · Diane T's 1/2-inch (13mm) Petal · Loew-Cornell No. 2 Flat · Loew-Cornell No. 4 Flat · Loew-Cornell No. 8 Flat · Loew-Cornell No. 10 Flat · Loew-Cornell No. 12 Flat · Loew-Cornell 3/8-inch (10mm) Angle · Loew-Cornell 1/2-inch (13mm) Angle · Loew-Cornell 5/8-inch (16mm) Angle

Basic Painting Techniques

DOUBLE LOADING AN ANGLE BRUSH

One Load one corner of the brush into the darker color and the other corner into the lighter color. ■

Two Blend on your palette to work the two colors up into the bristles. Keep the same colors on the same sides. ■

DOUBLE LOADING AN ANGEL WING BRUSH

One Load one side of the brush into the darker color and the other side into the lighter color. ■

Two Blend the colors, wiping off excess color onto a paper towel, and tap the brush onto your surface. ■

LOADING A BRUSH FOR FLOATING

One Dampen an angle brush in clean water. Pick up a corner load of paint on the toe, or long side, of the brush. ■

Two Stroke and blend on your palette until the edge is soft and fades gradually away. Apply the float to the design. ■

SCUMBLING

One To scumble means to apply paint in a rough, slip-slap motion. Start by applying your first color to your surface, working quickly to keep the paint wet. ■

Two Scumble in the second color to get a soft, textured effect. This must be done while the colors are still wet. Blend just enough that there are no lines of demarcation. You should still be able to see touches of each color. ■

TINTING LEAF EDGES AND BACKLIGHTING

Tinting the edges of leaves brings more color and interest to plain green leaves. After painting the leaves, add a float to part of the leaf edge with a red such as Deep Burgundy, Napthol Red or Cranberry Wine. ■

Tint the base or shaded part of the leaf with a dry brush of Violet Haze. Backlighting is done only in the dark areas to show reflected light on the leaf. Use this technique sparingly, not on every leaf in the design. ■

DE-GLAZING A GLAZED CERAMIC TILE

One To achieve a bisque finish on a glazed tile, apply a heavy coat of Etchall etching creme and let sit for 30 minutes. ■

Two Wash off the etching creme in the sink under running water. Compare the bisque side with the glazed side above. ■

Ripe Olives Trivet

Surface

6-inch (15.2cm) square ceramic tile in a black metal trivet, available at crafts supply stores. Plain square tile in various sizes available at any home improvement center.

Preparation

Tape off the edge of the tile with masking tape. Basecoat with Camel. Remove tape and basecoat the edges with Light Buttermilk. Paint a thin wiggly line of Avocado between the two colors. Let dry and transfer the pattern onto the tile using tracing paper and graphite paper.

Brushes

- 3/4-inch (19mm) glazing
- 1/2-inch (13mm) angle
- no. 10 flat
- small dome
- 10/0 striper
- nos. 2, 4 and 8 petal

Additional Supplies

- Masking tape
- Tracing paper
- Graphite paper
- J.W. etc. Matte Polyurethane Varnish

Perhaps you have decorated your kitchen with the old-world charm of Tuscany. This trivet tile is very simple to paint and would fit in well with the Tuscan theme. Try painting the same design on a vinegar-and-oil cruet set. ■

Paint DecoArt Americana Acrylics

| Camel | Light Buttermilk | Avocado | Burnt Umber | Evergreen | Olive Green | Cadmium Red | Deep Burgundy |

| Black Plum | Electric Pink | Admiral Blue | Payne's Grey |

Pattern

This pattern may be hand-traced or photocopied for personal use only. Enlarge at 147% to bring up to full size.

One

Base in the branch and stems with Burnt Umber on a no. 2 or 4 petal brush. Using a no. 8 petal brush, thin some Avocado with water and wash in the leaves. Load a 1/2-inch (13mm) angle brush with a float of Evergreen and shade the leaves.

Two

Highlight the leaves with Olive Green. Use a 10/0 striper and Olive Green to add the vein lines. Tint the leaves with Cadmium Red.

Three

Base in the red olives with Deep Burgundy on a no. 10 flat. While this is still wet, use a small dome brush to shade with a brush mix of Deep Burgundy and Black Plum.

Four

Highlight the red olives with Electric Pink. Tint them with Cadmium Red, and add a final highlight glint of Light Buttermilk. The black olives are based in with Admiral Blue. While this is wet, shade them with Payne's Grey.

Five

Highlight the black olives with a brush mix of Light Buttermilk and Admiral Blue. Tint each black olive with Cadmium Red. The highlight glint is Light Buttermilk.

QUICK TIP

Want to achieve highlights that are softer and less structured? Lightly stipple in the highlights with your brush, then tap them with your finger while they're still wet to soften.

FINISHING

Add a shadow underneath or next to each leaf, olive and stem with a wash of Burnt Umber on a no. 8 petal brush. Let dry.

To protect the painted tile, varnish with at least two coats of matte varnish; allow to dry between coats.

Floral Address Tiles

Surface
4-inch (10.2cm) square ceramic tiles in a black metal frame from Ceramics and Crafts Warehouse (see Resources). Plain square tiles in various sizes also available at any home improvement center.

Preparation
Basecoat the tiles entirely with J.W. etc. UnderCover. When dry, basecoat again with Light Buttermilk. Let dry and transfer the patterns onto the tiles using tracing paper and graphite paper.

Brushes
- 3/4-inch (19mm) glazing
- no. 8 flat
- 10/0 striper
- no. 2 petal

Additional Supplies
- Masking tape or painter's tape
- Tracing paper
- Graphite paper
- J.W. etc. UnderCover (white)
- J.W. etc. Matte Polyurethane Varnish

What an attractive first impression these address tiles will make on your front porch! A couple coats of varnish will protect them from the weather. There are many styles of numbers available either as stencils at the craft stores or as fonts on your computer. ■

Paint DecoArt Americana Acrylics

Light Buttermilk · Soft Black · Avocado · Olive Green

Cadmium Yellow · Burnt Sienna · Antique Mauve

Pattern

These patterns may be hand-traced or photocopied for
personal use only. They are shown here full size.

One

After tracing and transferring the pattern onto each address tile, load a no. 8 flat brush with Soft Black and paint the number. Let dry, and apply a second coat of Soft Black for even coverage.

Two

Using a 10/0 striper and Avocado, paint the vine that winds up and around each number. Follow the pattern or freehand the vine in a design you like. You may need a second coat of Avocado where the vine crosses over top of the number.

Three

Double load a no. 2 petal brush with Avocado and Olive Green. Place a few tiny leaves along the vine — not too many, you'll be adding more after the flowers are painted. Double load the no. 2 petal with Cadmium Yellow and Burnt Sienna and dot in the centers for the flowers along the vine.

Four

Double load a no. 2 petal brush with Antique Mauve and Light Buttermilk. Pull little daisy petals out from the centers you placed along the vine in step 3. Keep the Antique Mauve to the same side on each petal to act as shading. You may need to repeat over the black number for good coverage.

Five

Add a tiny highlight dot of Light Buttermilk in the daisy centers using a 10/0 striper. Shade the bottom of the centers with Burnt Sienna. Add more leaves around the flowers using a double-load of Olive Green and Avocado on a no. 2 petal brush. Repeat if needed for good coverage over the number.

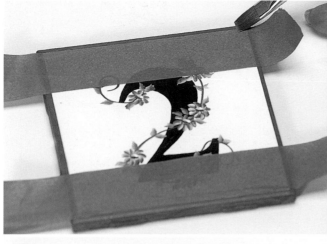

Six

Tape off the outer edge of each tile with masking tape or blue painter's tape, leaving about a 1/4-inch (6mm) margin. Paint the edges with Avocado on a no. 8 flat, carrying the color over the entire edge and onto the back of the tile. Remove the tape before the paint dries.

Seven

Let your painted address tiles dry completely, and check to be sure each number is clearly visible.

FINISHING

To protect your painted tiles from the weather, be sure to apply at least two coats of a matte polyurethane varnish, letting dry between coats.

The tiles may be mounted directly to your front door, wall or porch, using epoxy glue. Or you can mount them in a wooden or metal frame. This black metal frame from Ceramics and Crafts Warehouse (see the Resources section on page 126) comes in several lengths to accommodate long and short address numbers.

Lemon Topiary

MATERIALS

Surface
16-inch (40.6cm) square ceramic floor tile with a slightly textured surface, available at any home improvement center or tile and flooring store. Ask them to cut the tile in half for you.

Preparation
Wipe off the tile with a soft cloth. Trace and transfer the pattern.

Brushes
- no. 10 flat
- 10/0 rake
- 1/2-inch (13mm) angle
- 3/4-inch (19mm) glazing
- 10/0 striper
- nos. 4 and 8 petal

Additional Supplies
- Tracing paper
- Graphite paper
- Krylon 18k Gold Leafing Pen
- Brown shoe polish
- Krylon Matte Finish spray
- Delta Ceramcoat 2-Step Fine Crackle Finish
- Soft cloth

This was a large 16-inch (40.6cm) square ceramic floor tile that I had cut in half. The vertical shape enhances the tall lemon topiary tree, and the fine crackle finish I applied after the painting was done really sets off the old-world look. This tile can be placed in a stand or hung on a wall. ▪

Paint DecoArt Americana Acrylics

Terra Cotta | Burnt Umber | Hauser Dark Green | Jade Green | Soft Black | Light Buttermilk | Burnt Sienna | Violet Haze

Napthol Red | Cadmium Yellow | Avocado | Limeade | Antique Gold | Pineapple | Emperor's Gold

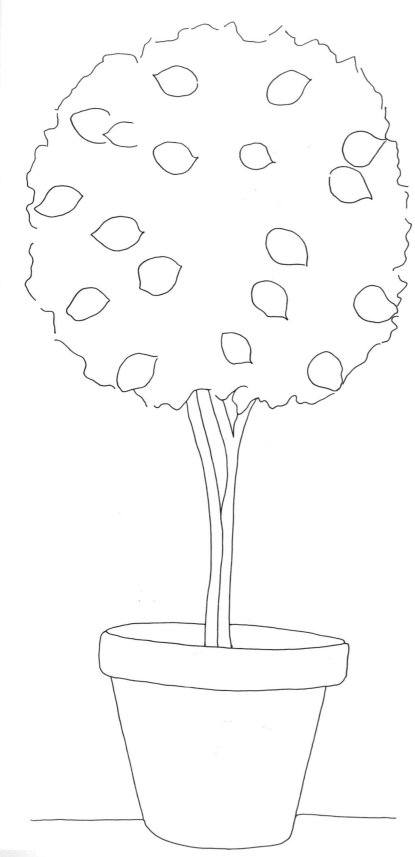

Pattern

This pattern may be hand-traced or photocopied for personal use only. Enlarge at 161% to bring up to full size.

One

Base in the pot with Terra Cotta on a no. 10 flat. Paint the trunks with a no. 4 petal brush and Burnt Umber. Scumble in the topiary ball first with Hauser Dark Green, then with Jade Green.

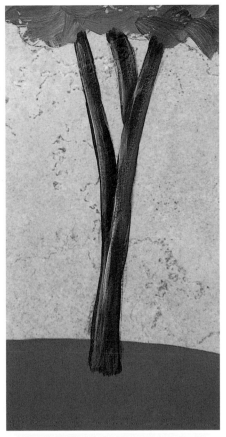

Two

Shade the trunks with Soft Black on the right sides, and highlight the left sides with Light Buttermilk.

Three

Shade the right side and under the rim of the terra cotta pot with Burnt Sienna. Highlight the left side with Light Buttermilk.

Darken the inside ellipse of the pot with Burnt Umber. Darken the shading along the right side and under the rim with a float of Burnt Umber on a 1/2-inch (13mm) angle brush. Let dry. Backlight the shaded areas with Violet Haze. Tint the dark side with Napthol Red and the light side with Cadmium Yellow. Highlight the edge of the pot rim with a fine line of Light Buttermilk on a 10/0 striper.

Four

23

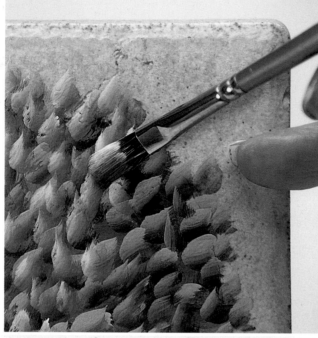

Five

Double load a no. 8 petal brush with Hauser Dark Green and Jade Green. Paint the first layer of leaves. Let dry. Double load the brush with Avocado and Limeade and add some lighter leaves mostly on the top and along the side to highlight the topiary ball.

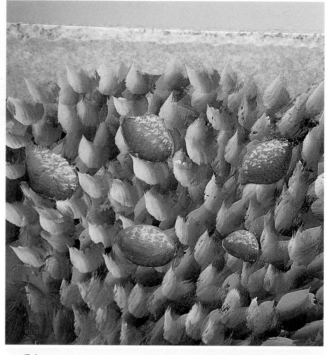

Six

Base in the lemons with Antique Gold on a no. 4 petal. Shade the underside of each lemon with Burnt Sienna on a 1/2-inch (13mm) angle. Load the corner of a 10/0 rake with Pineapple and stipple in highlights along the top side of each lemon.

Seven

QUICK TIP

There is no need to paint the first layer of leaves too carefully because they will be mostly covered up. Only the last layer of leaves will show.

Tint the lemons with Cadmium Yellow on the light sides. Tint the shaded sides with Napthol Red. To set the lemons back into the leaves, pull a few more leaves overlapping the lemons using the same colors as in step 5.

FINISHING

Place a few Violet Haze leaves in the darker side of the topiary ball using a no. 8 petal brush. Wash in a shadow under the pot with thinned Burnt Umber and a few streaks of Violet Haze for a backlight.

Around the edge of the tile, finish off with a band of 18k gold leafing pen, or with Emperor's Gold paint and a brush.

If you wish, add a crackled finish to the tile when all the paint is completely dry. Following the manufacturer's instructions, apply a heavy coat of Step 1 of the Fine Crackle Finish, using a 3/4-inch (19mm) glazing brush. Let this dry. Apply Step 2 of the Fine Crackle Finish and let dry. Using a soft cloth, rub brown shoe polish on the surface until you see the crackling appear. Wipe off any excess.

To protect your painted tile, spray on a matte varnish to seal the surface.

Raspberry Trivet

MATERIALS

Surface
6-inch (15.2cm) round ceramic tile in a round trivet from Ceramics and Crafts Warehouse (see Resources on page 126). Plain round tile also available at any arts and crafts supply store.

Preparation
Wipe off the tile with a soft cloth. Apply the first basecoat of Light Buttermilk to the entire tile and let dry.

Brushes
- 1/2-inch (13mm) angle
- 3/4-inch (19mm) glazing
- 10/0 striper
- nos. 2 and 8 petal

Additional Supplies
- Tracing paper
- Graphite paper
- Natural sea sponge
- Loew-Cornell Medium Berry Maker
- J.W. etc. Matte Polyurethane Varnish

What a pretty addition this would make to your breakfast table, along with a jar of fruit preserves and some hot biscuits! This round ceramic tile is easy and fun to paint using a new foam applicator called a Berry Maker. You can make luscious looking berries like these in seconds. ■

Paint DecoArt Americana Acrylics

Light Buttermilk   Deep Burgundy   Burnt Umber   Boysenberry Pink   Red Violet   Royal Purple

Olive Green   Avocado   Evergreen   Violet Haze   Emperor's Gold

Pattern

This pattern may be hand-traced or photocopied for personal use only. It is shown here full size.

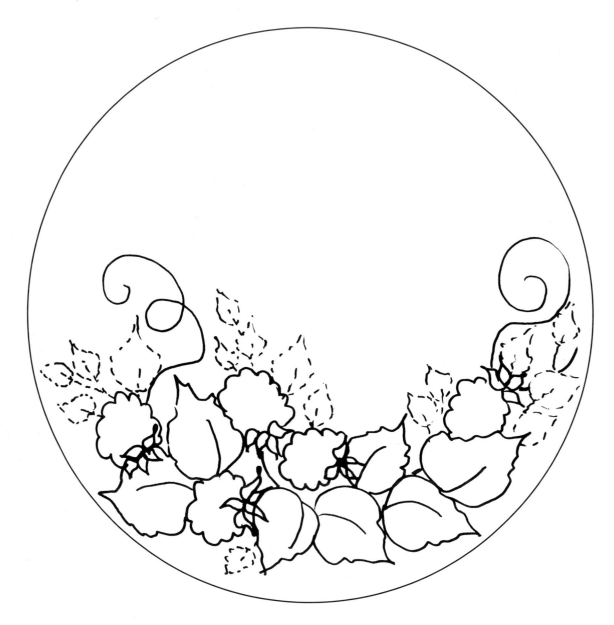

One

With a dampened natural sea sponge, dab on some Light Buttermilk on the entire front of the tile. While it is still wet, turn your sponge to a clean area, pick up some Deep Burgundy and dab this color in a crescent moon shape, letting the pink color fade out gradually toward the center as shown. Let this dry, then trace and transfer the pattern onto the tile.

Two

Load a 10/0 striper with Deep Burgundy and a touch of Burnt Umber, and place in the vine, following the curve of the tile. Don't worry if your vine isn't perfect—it will be mostly covered by berries and leaves as you go.

Three

There are many ways to paint raspberries, but for this project I used a foam dabbing tool called a Berry Maker, which makes painting berries quick and easy. Practice on some scrap paper first to get the feel of it. To paint the pink berries on the tile, load a medium Berry Maker into Boysenberry Pink, tap out the excess on your palette, and dab a few berry segments onto your tile.

Four

To shade the pink berries, load the Berry Maker into Deep Burgundy, tap out the excess on your palette, and dab in the rest of the berry segments. You'll see that the Berry Maker automatically places the little ring around each segment. As you dab, allow the segments to overlap and build into a rounded raspberry shape.

Five

Since raspberries turn many colors as they ripen, I've added some purple berries to the branch. Load the medium Berry Maker into Red Violet, tap out the excess, and dab on a few berry segments.

Six

Then load the Berry Maker into Royal Purple and dab on the rest of the segments.

Seven

When all the berries are dry, load a 1/2-inch (13mm) angle brush with a float of Olive Green, and indicate a few areas where the berries aren't quite ripe yet.

Eight

Raspberries have a shiny skin on each segment, so to make your berries look a little more realistic, load a 10/0 striper with Light Buttermilk and place a tiny highlight glint on each segment of each berry. Be sure to keep the highlights all on one side and facing the light source.

Nine

Load a no. 8 petal brush with thinned Avocado and place in the larger leaf shapes. Paint around the berries, but paint right over the stem. Wiggle the petal brush to make the leaf edges look curved.

Ten

Shade each larger leaf with Evergreen and highlight with Olive Green. Place in the vein lines with Olive Green on a 10/0 striper. Load a 1/2-inch (13mm) angle with a float of Deep Burgundy and tint a few leaf edges.

Eleven

Double load a no. 2 petal brush with Olive Green and Evergreen and add a calyx (or hull) to each berry. Backlight the darker areas of the leaves with a little Violet Haze on a no. 8 petal brush.

Twelve

Thin some Avocado with water and place in some small filler leaves here and there among the berries. Then place a few background leaves with thinned Violet Haze. Load a 10/0 striper with Avocado and pull stems into the leaves, then finish with some curly tendrils at either end of the raspberry branch.

FINISHING

To finish off the round tile, load a 1/2-inch (13mm) angle brush with Emperor's Gold and paint the edge of the design and the edge of the tile itself. Take your time and do this freehand, and don't worry if it isn't exactly perfect. If you get too much gold paint on the front, just take a damp paper towel or cotton swab and lift it off while it's still wet. The round metal trivet was originally black, so I painted it with Emperor's Gold to match the tile. Or it can be spray painted with gold paint. To protect the painted tile, apply at least two coats of a matte polyurethane varnish, letting it dry between coats.

Pear, Plum & Cherries Tile

Here is an easy tile project for your kitchen—the colorful fruits will complement almost any decorating style. To give this tile an aged, almost faded look, I used a crackle medium over the painting with a final rub of white oil paint. ■

MATERIALS

Surface
6-inch (15.2cm) square white ceramic tile with matte or glazed finish, available at any home improvement center or tile and flooring store.

Preparation
If your tile is glazed, remove the glazing first (see page 9). Basecoat the tile with J.W. etc. UnderCover.

Brushes
- 1/2-inch (13mm) angle
- 5/8-inch (16 mm) angle
- 3/4-inch (19mm) glazing
- medium dome brush
- no. 12 flat
- no. 8 petal
- 10/0 striper

Additional Supplies
- Etchall etching creme (optional)
- J.W. etc. UnderCover (white)
- Blue painter's tape
- Delta Ceramcoat 2-Step Fine Crackle Finish
- White oil or acrylic paint
- J.W. etc. Texture Gel Glaze (optional)
- Krylon Matte Finish spray
- J.W. etc. Matte Polyurethane Varnish (optional)

Paint DecoArt Americana Acrylics

Light Buttermilk | Cadmium Yellow | Plum | Napthol Red | Soft Sage | Raw Sienna | Burnt Umber

Tangelo Orange | Violet Haze | Black Plum | Avocado | Peony Pink | Deep Burgundy

Pattern

This pattern may be hand-traced or photocopied
for personal use only. It is shown here full size.

One

Basecoat the tile with Light Buttermilk. Let dry and transfer the pattern. With a no. 8 petal brush, base in the pear with Cadmium Yellow, the plum with Plum, and the cherries with Napthol Red. Base in the leaves with Soft Sage.

Two

Load a 5/8-inch (16mm) angle with a float of Raw Sienna and shade the pear as shown. Highlight the pear's center with Light Buttermilk on a medium dome brush. Paint the stem with Burnt Umber and highlight with Light Buttermilk. Wash in the shadow under the fruit with thinned Burnt Umber, softening and fading out the edges with a clean damp brush.

Three

The second layer of shading on the pear is a brush mix of Tangelo Orange and Burnt Umber. Tint the darker areas with Napthol Red. Add a Violet Haze backlight here and there in the shaded areas. Add the final highlight to the lightest parts of the pear with Light Buttermilk.

Four

On the plum, shade around the edges with a float of Black Plum on a 5/8-inch (16mm) angle brush. Let dry. Highlight the center area with a brush mix of Plum and Light Buttermilk. Line in a stem with Burnt Umber, highlighted with Light Buttermilk.

Five

Glaze the entire plum with thinned Napthol Red to warm it up. Add a backlight of Violet Haze in the shaded area. The sharp highlight is a comma stroke of Light Buttermilk. Shade the leaves with a float of Avocado on a 1/2-inch (13mm) angle brush. Line in the veins with Avocado, and tint the upper edge of the leaves with a float of Napthol Red.

Six

Begin the first highlight color on the cherries with Peony Pink on a medium dome brush. Shade each cherry with a float of Deep Burgundy on a 1/2-inch (13mm) angle brush. Shade again with a float of Black Plum, and indicate the stem indentations.

Seven

Tint here and there on the cherries with a wash of Tangelo Orange. Add a backlight of Violet Haze in the shaded area of each cherry and in between to separate them. Load a 10/0 striper with Light Buttermilk and add a highlight glint to each cherry.

Eight

The pear leaves and cherry leaves are painted in the same way. Shade them with a float of Avocado on a 1/2-inch (13mm) angle brush. Add vein lines with Avocado on a 10/0 striper. Tint the lighter areas of the leaves with Cadmium Yellow.

Nine

Finish the leaves by floating a little Napthol Red along one edge, and adding a backlight of Violet Haze in the darker areas. Paint a tendril from the stem of the pear outward with Avocado on a 10/0 striper.

FINISHING

Tape off the edges of the tile, leaving a 1/4-inch (6mm) margin along the outside edge. Load a no. 12 flat with Avocado and paint the edges. Remove the tape before the paint dries.

If you wish to crackle the tile as shown here, make sure all the paint is completely dry. Following the manufacturer's instructions, apply a 2-step fine crackle finish. Let this dry, then spray the tile with Krylon Matte Finish.

To achieve the faded look, rub a little white oil paint into the crackle with a soft cloth, then wipe off. When dry, varnish the tile with another coat of matte spray finish. Or for a more durable finish, apply a couple of coats of matte polyurethane varnish, letting dry between coats.

Four Floral Tin Tiles

T hese four floral designs are painted on reproductions of old-fashioned tin ceiling tiles. I chose a very simple embossed (or raised) design which acts as a built-in frame around each flower. Group the four painted tiles over your mantle or on the wall for a cottage-style home accent. ■

MATERIALS

Surface
12-inch (30.5cm) square tin ceiling tile from Viking Woodcrafts. Other styles available at craft stores and home improvement centers.

Preparation
Basecoat the front of each tile with two coats of white J.W. etc. UnderCover. This gives tooth to the tin surface for your paints to adhere to.

Brushes
- 1/2-inch (13mm) angle
- 3/8-inch (10mm) angle
- 3/4-inch (19mm) glazing
- no. 12 flat
- nos. 4 and 8 petal
- 1/2-inch (13mm) petal
- 10/0 striper

Additional Supplies
- J.W. etc. UnderCover (white)
- Tracing paper
- Graphite paper
- J.W. etc. Matte Polyurethane Varnish

Paint DecoArt Americana Acrylics

| Light Buttermilk | Soft Sage | Hauser Med. Green | Evergreen | Olive Green | Cranberry Wine | Country Blue | Burnt Sienna |
| Cadmium Yellow | Emperor's Gold | Hi-Lite Flesh | Napthol Red | Royal Purple | Boysenberry Pink | Titanium White | |

Coneflowers

Pattern

This pattern may be hand-traced or photocopied for personal use only. Enlarge at 115% to bring up to full size.

BACKGROUND AND LEAVES

One

Scumble in the green background in the center of the tin tile with Soft Sage and Light Buttermilk. The upper right corner is lighter in value than the lower left. When dry, transfer the pattern to the tile. If you are painting all four floral tiles in this project, paint the same background for all four.

Two

Load a no. 4 petal brush with Hauser Medium Green and line in the stems. Thin this color with water and place in the leaves with a no. 8 petal brush. Shade the base of the leaves with a float of Evergreen. Add vein lines with Evergreen on a 10/0 striper. Highlight with thinned Olive Green; tint some edges with Cranberry Wine; and backlight with Country Blue.

Three

With a no. 8 petal, base in the flower centers with Burnt Sienna. Stroke on the coneflower petals with a mix of Cranberry Wine and Light Buttermilk. When dry, float a shade of Cranberry Wine over the base of the petals. Add vein lines of Cranberry Wine using a 10/0 striper, and tint the outside edges of the petals with a float of Country Blue.

Four

With a no. 4 petal, stipple the flower centers using Burnt Sienna and Cadmium Yellow wet-on-wet. Float a small shade of Country Blue at the base of the cone. The seeds at the base of the cone are dotted in with a soft black mixed from Cranberry Wine and Evergreen on a 10/0 striper.

FINISHING

Outline the center design area of the tin tile with a band of Emperor's Gold on a no. 12 flat. The light green bands in the white area of the tile are painted with thinned Hauser Medium Green.

When all the paint is dry, protect your tile with at least two coats of matte polyurethane varnish.

Hydrangea

Pattern

This pattern may be hand-traced or photocopied for personal use only. Enlarge at 143% to bring up to full size.

BACKGROUND AND FLORETS

One

Scumble in the green background in the center of the tin tile with Soft Sage and Light Buttermilk. The upper right corner is lighter in value than the lower left. When dry, transfer the pattern to the tile. With a 1/2-inch (13mm) petal brush, slip-slap Cranberry Wine into the area of the hydrangea blossom. Use a lot of paint because you will be working wet-on-wet. Load a no. 8 petal brush with Hi-Lite Flesh and paint the four-petal florets. Reload your brush for every floret; do not rinse your brush in water, just wipe off excess paint on a paper towel. Dot in the centers of each floret with Olive Green.

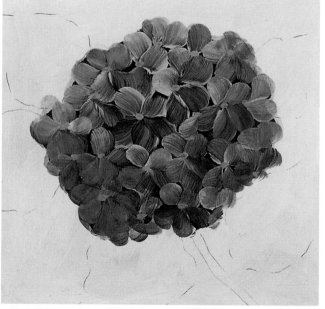

Two

Dab on a wash of thinned Cranberry Wine to shade the lower half of the blossom. Dab in some backlighting with Country Blue. Tint the upper half of the blossom with a thinned wash of Napthol Red. Dab in a little bit of thinned Cadmium Yellow to warm up and highlight the petals.

Three

Base in the leaves and stems with Hauser Medium Green on a no. 8 petal brush. Where the two leaves overlap the hydrangea blossom, add another coat for good coverage. Shade the base of the leaves and the center vein area with Evergreen corner-loaded onto a 1/2-inch (13mm) angle brush. Tint the lighter areas of the leaves with a wash of Cadmium Yellow. Load a 10/0 striper with Olive Green and paint the vein lines. Tint some of the leaf edges with a float of Cranberry Wine on a 1/2-inch (13mm) angle brush. Let dry.

FINISHING

Outline the center design area of the tin tile with a band of Emperor's Gold on a no. 12 flat. The light green bands in the white area of the tile are painted with thinned Hauser Medium Green.

When all the paint is dry, protect your tile with at least two coats of matte polyurethane varnish.

Roses

Pattern

This pattern may be hand-traced or photocopied for personal use only. Enlarge at 141% to bring up to full size.

RED AND PURPLE ROSE PETALS

One

Scumble in the green background in the center of the tin tile with Soft Sage and Light Buttermilk. The upper right corner is lighter in value than the lower left. When dry, transfer the pattern to the tile. Scumble in the red rose with Cranberry Wine. Double load a 1/2-inch (13mm) angle with Cranberry Wine and Light Buttermilk and paint the back petals of the bud area. Pull the front petals of the bud, then the open petals, keeping the lighter color toward the outside edge. Tint the petals with thinned Cadmium Yellow; tint the deeper parts with thinned Napthol Red. Begin the purple rose by blocking in the shape with a scumble of Royal Purple.

Two

Double load a 3/8-inch (10mm) angle brush into Royal Purple and Light Buttermilk. Stroke in the back petals of the bud area with short, slightly curved brushstrokes. Pull the larger petals of the cup from each side in toward the center, keeping the Light Buttermilk to the top edges.

With the same colors and brush, paint the open petals of the purple rose, pulling short strokes from each side. Tint the petals with Cranberry Wine thinned with water. Dot in seeds in the centers of both roses with Emperor's Gold and a 10/0 striper.

Three

FINISHING

Begin the leaves by dabbing in Hauser Medium Green using a no. 8 petal brush. Let dry, and shade the leaves with a corner load of Evergreen on a 1/2-inch (13mm) angle brush. Paint vein lines with Olive Green on a 10/0 striper. Tint the edges of the leaves with a float of Cranberry Wine. Wash a little Cadmium Yellow into the lighter areas of each leaf. Let dry and add a touch of Napthol Red to the leaves. With a no. 8 petal, drybrush some Country Blue backlighting onto the shaded areas of the leaves. Finish with some tendrils drawn in with a 10/0 striper and Hauser Medium Green.

Outline the center design area of the tin tile with a band of Emperor's Gold on a no. 12 flat. The light green bands in the white area of the tile are painted with thinned Hauser Medium Green.

When all the paint is dry, protect your tile with at least two coats of matte polyurethane varnish.

Wildflowers

Pattern

This pattern may be hand-traced or photocopied for personal use only. Enlarge at 139% to bring up to full size.

BACKGROUND AND LEAVES

One

Scumble in the green background in the center of the tin tile with Soft Sage and Light Buttermilk. The upper right corner is lighter in value than the lower left. When dry, transfer the pattern to the tile. Darken the lower left corner of the center green square with Hauser Medium Green. Load this same color on a no. 8 petal brush and paint the subtle shadow leaves in the background. Tint the tips and edges of the leaves with thinned Cranberry Wine. Load a 10/0 striper with Evergreen and add the vein lines.

Two

Line in the wildflower stems with Evergreen on a 10/0 striper. Paint the flower bases with Hauser Medium Green, then dot in some Evergreen. The calyxes and darker leaves are placed in with thinned Evergreen.

Three

The purple flower's center is Country Blue. While this color is still wet, double load a 10/0 striper with Royal Purple and Titanium White and pull the spiky petals out from the center. Alternate picking up those two colors so the petals are varied in color. Pull out a few spikes of Boysenberry Pink. Shade the center with Royal Purple and tap in tiny dots of Cadmium Yellow for seeds.

The pink flower's center is Cranberry Wine. While the center is still wet, double load a 10/0 striper with Boysenberry Pink and Titanium White and pull spiky petals out from the center, alternating between the pink and the white. Pull a few petals of Royal Purple.

FINISHING

Shade along the pink flower's center with Cranberry Wine, then dot in a few seeds in the center with Cadmium Yellow.

Outline the center design area of the tin tile with a band of Emperor's Gold on a no. 12 flat. The light green bands in the white area of the tile are painted with thinned Hauser Medium Green.

When all the paint is dry, protect your tile with at least two coats of matte polyurethane varnish.

Le Vin Grenache

MATERIALS

Surface
16-inch (40.6cm) square ceramic floor tile cut in half, available at any home improvement center or tile and flooring store.

Preparation
Wipe off tile with clean cloth. Trace and transfer the pattern, except for the lettering.

Brushes
- nos. 4 and 10 flat
- 3/4-inch (19 mm) glazing
- 5/8-inch (16mm) angle
- 1/2-inch (13mm) angle
- nos. 2, 4 and 8 petal
- 10/0 striper

Additional Supplies
- Tracing paper
- Graphite paper
- Brown permanent ink pen
- Krylon 18k Gold Leafing Pen (optional)
- Gloss polyurethane varnish

A bottle of good wine and a loaf of crusty bread—what a great way to pass an evening at "le bistro." This wine-and-grapes design was painted on a large square ceramic floor tile that I had cut in half to make a vertical tile. I repeated the grape cluster on a glass bottle with a wick for the soft glow of candlelight. ■

Paint DecoArt Americana Acrylics

| Green Mist | Buttermilk | Cranberry Wine | Emperor's Gold | Sable Brown | Plum | Hauser Med. Green | Black Green | Hauser Dark Green | Yellow Green |

| Country Blue | Asphaltum | Black Plum | Burnt Sienna | Napthol Red | Boysenberry Pink | Grey Sky | Graphite | Titanium White |

Pattern

This pattern may be hand-traced or photocopied for personal use only. Enlarge at 129% to bring up to full size.

Reserva Reser

Domaine
Chardoney
1990
Vinyards

BASECOAT

One

Using a no. 10 flat, basecoat the wine bottle with Green Mist, and the labels with Buttermilk. The top sealer band is Cranberry Wine, the narrow band underneath is Emperor's Gold, and the cork is Sable Brown. Base in the grapes loosely with Plum and the wine in the glass with Cranberry Wine. The grape leaves are loosely based in with Hauser Medium Green.

Two

With a 5/8-inch (16mm) angle brush, float the first shade on the wine bottle with Hauser Dark Green, following the outside contours of the bottle. Shade above and below the labels also.

Three

When the first shading is dry, float a second shade using Black Green along the right side of the bottle. Tint the center areas of the bottle with a wash of Yellow Green. Float a backlight of Country Blue into the darkest shade areas.

Four

On the large label, base in the roses with thinned Cranberry Wine on a no. 4 petal. While this is still wet, use unthinned Cranberry Wine to shade and define the little rose petals. Paint the leaves with Hauser Medium Green; thin this color and paint the tiny ferns. Load a 10/0 striper with Emperor's Gold and draw in the horizontal lines on the upper and lower labels. Shade both labels with a float of thinned Asphaltum. Let dry, and reshade the right sides of the labels with Asphaltum. Base in the emblem on the top label with Asphaltum and draw crosshatch lines with Emperor's Gold. To make the label edges look ragged, line the edges with Asphaltum on a 10/0 striper.

QUICK TIP

Sometimes it's a little tricky getting the shape of a bottle or glass even on both sides. Try turning your tile upside down after you have based in the shapes and looking at them from the top down. You'll be able to spot any unevenness more easily.

Five

Backlight the right sides of both labels with thinned Country Blue. Shade the individual grapes with a float of thinned Black Plum on a 1/2-inch (13mm) angle brush. On the side of each grape opposite the shaded side, highlight with a float of Boysenberry Pink. This is what gives roundness to each grape.

Six

Tint the center of each grape with a little thinned Napthol Red. Backlight the bottom of some of the grapes with a float of Country Blue. Do not take this float all the way to the edge of the grape or you will cover up the shading. Place a tiny highlight glint on each grape with Buttermilk on a 10/0 striper.

Seven

The grape leaves are shaded with Hauser Dark Green, then highlighted with Green Mist. Tint the highlighted areas with a wash of Yellow Green.

Eight

Float a little Cranberry Wine on the edge of each leaf. Place vein lines with Hauser Dark Green on a 10/0 striper. Tint the shaded areas with a wash of Country Blue. Load a 10/0 striper with Hauser Dark Green and line in the tendrils coming off each side of the grape cluster.

Nine

Wash in the clear glass area of the wine glass with thinned Grey Sky. Follow the pattern lines and avoid painting over the wine you have already based in. Paint the stem of the wine glass too.

Ten

To make the wine look like it is inside the glass, shade with a float of Black Plum on a 1/2-inch (13mm) angle brush. Follow the shape of the bottom of the wine glass, and float a curving shade where the top of the wine touches the inside front of the glass.

Eleven

Warm up the wine's color with a tint of Napthol Red. Load a 10/0 striper with Titanium White and outline the top of the wine with a hit-and-miss line. Shade the wine glass with a float of thinned Graphite around the top rim, along the sides of the bowl and stem, and back of the base. Line the base front with Graphite and tint with thinned Cranberry Wine.

Twelve

To show reflection of light on the wine glass, pull curving highlights of Titanium White along both sides of the bowl. With Titanium White on a 10/0 striper, outline the top edge of the glass, and highlight the left side of the stem and base. Tint the highlights with a thin wash of Country Blue.

Thirteen

To finish the labels, transfer the lettering on the pattern to your tile. Use a brown permanent ink pen to draw in the lettering on the upper and lower labels.

Fourteen

QUICK TIP

When painting distinct edges on objects like the wine bottle and glass in this project, sometimes the paint will stray onto the background. I don't stop and clean up my background as I paint. I wait until I am finished with the painting, then go back and scrape off any edges of paint I don't want. The smooth, hard surface of the tile makes it easy to do this.

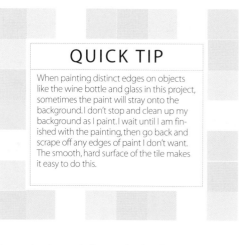

On the sealer under the cork, float a shade of Black Plum. Shade both sides of the gold band with Burnt Sienna. Shade the cork with Asphaltum, and highlight the top edge with thinned Buttermilk. Lighten the center of the sealer band with a tint of Napthol Red. Place a highlight stroke of Buttermilk on the left side.

FINISHING

Finish the wine bottle with a vertical hit-and-miss highlight of Buttermilk on the left side to show reflection of light on the glass.

Transfer the pattern of the wine bottle and glass to the tile, offsetting it to the right of the painted areas for cast shadows in the background. Paint the shadows with a thinned wash of Asphaltum. Use a 5/8-inch (16mm) angle brush to float Asphaltum shadows under the bottle, grapes, and glass.

Finish the edges of the tile with a band of gold, using either Emperor's Gold and a brush, or an 18k gold leafing pen. Let dry.

Protect your painted tile with two coats of gloss polyurethane varnish.

Papa Bird Wall Pocket

MATERIALS

Surface
12-inch (30.5cm) square wall pocket made with two tin ceiling tiles, available from Painters Paradise.

Preparation
Use a 3/4-inch (19mm) glazing brush and basecoat the entire piece with J.W. etc. UnderCover. Let dry, and re-basecoat with Light Buttermilk.

Brushes
- 1/2-inch (13mm) angle
- 3/4-inch (19mm) glazing
- 1/2-inch (13mm) petal
- nos. 2, 4 and 8 petal
- 10/0 striper

Additional Supplies
- J.W. etc. UnderCover (white)
- Blue painter's tape
- Tracing paper
- Graphite paper
- J.W. etc. Gold Metallic Wax (optional)
- Cotton swabs
- J.W. etc. Matte Polyurethane Varnish

Here is a fun project for a sunroom or outdoors on the patio. It's made of two embossed tin ceiling tiles attached together with wire to make a pocket. Try stuffing the pocket with nesting materials for the birds to pick out, or with dried or silk flowers for a year-round reminder of spring. ■

Paint DecoArt Americana Acrylics

Light Buttermilk	Hi-Lite Flesh	Burnt Umber	Soft Black	Violet Haze	Camel	Raw Sienna

Brandy Wine	Cadmium Yellow	Jade Green	Evergreen	Yellow Green	Emperor's Gold

Pattern

This pattern may be hand-traced or photocopied for personal use only. Enlarge at 105% to bring up to full size.

BACKGROUND AND BRANCHES

One

Tape off the edges around the center with blue painter's tape. Using a 1/2-inch (13mm) petal brush, scumble on the background colors of Light Buttermilk, Hi-Lite Flesh and Burnt Umber, making it darker in the lower left corner and fading out toward the upper right. Use plenty of paint to prevent lines of demarcation. Smooth out the scumble with thinned Burnt Umber. Let dry and transfer the pattern.

Two

Use a no. 4 petal brush to place in the main branches, working wet-on-wet. Start with Burnt Umber, and while this is wet, high-light with Hi-Lite Flesh and shade with Soft Black. The smaller branches and twigs are lined in with Burnt Umber on a 10/0 striper. Add a little Violet Haze on the dark side for a backlight.

TAIL FEATHERS

Three

Start painting the back tail feathers of the bird first. The first layer is based in with Burnt Umber. The shade is Soft Black and the lighter color is Camel. Use a no. 4 petal brush to create the tail feathers, staying up on the chisel edge of the brush sometimes, and using the flat of the brush other times.

Four

Using the same colors and brush, paint the next set of feathers that overlap the tail feathers on either side.

BIRD'S BREAST AND HEAD

Five

Load a no. 8 petal brush with Camel and stroke in the breast area. While this color is wet, stroke in some Burnt Umber along the outside edge of the breast. Then stroke in some Light Buttermilk in the Camel area. Your brush strokes should follow the direction of feather growth.

Six

Double load a no. 4 petal brush with Burnt Umber and Soft Black. Paint the throat feathers under the beak, working around the outline of the beak. Where these feathers overlap the breast, blend them in with some small strokes of Camel. Base in the bird's head with Camel, and shade with Burnt Umber to define the shape. Highlight with Light Buttermilk wet-on-wet. Put a touch of Soft Black around the beak and under the eye.

MAIN WING

Seven

Begin the main wing with Camel and Light Buttermilk in the center. Stroke in Burnt Umber along the edges of the wing and around the neck.

Eight

Shade along the wing's edges with short strokes of Soft Black. Blend the neck area wet-on-wet so there is not a harsh line. Add a little Raw Sienna to warm up the colors on the wing, head and tail feathers, and on the breast.

Nine

Base in the beak with Camel. Shade the beak and add the dividing line and nostril with Burnt Umber on a 10/0 striper. Use the same brush and Light Buttermilk to add thin highlight lines. Base in the eye with Soft Black, and add the reflective highlights with two little dots of Light Buttermilk.

Ten

To warm up the colors even further, float Brandy Wine mainly along the breast, but also on top of the head and into the feathers. Highlight the tips of the wing and tail feathers with a brush mix of Camel and Light Buttermilk. Warm up and tint the lighter areas of the bird with a wash of Cadmium Yellow, and the darker areas with a wash of Violet Haze. Paint in the feet with Burnt Umber and a little Light Buttermilk.

LEAVES

Eleven

Double load a no. 8 petal brush with Jade Green and Evergreen. Blend on your palette and make little one-stroke leaves coming off the branches. Wiggle your brush to create serrated edges, and keep the lighter green to the same side for each leaf. Let dry.

Twelve

Wash thinned Yellow Green into the lightest areas of the leaves. Let dry. Line in the veins with Evergreen on a 10/0 striper. Using a 1/2-inch (13mm) angle brush, float a tint of Brandy Wine on some of the leaf edges. Add backlighting to the darker areas of some of the leaves with Violet Haze. Connect the leaves to the branches with stems of Evergreen.

PINK FLOWERS

With a no. 2 or no. 4 petal brush, begin the flowers with Light Buttermilk for the lighter petals and Brandy Wine for the dark pink petals. Place in plenty of paint and work wet-on-wet. Let dry. You may need to reinforce the darker color by tucking some into the centers and at the bases of the flowers. At the bottom of each blossom, backlight with Violet Haze. Finish with tiny dots of Cadmium Yellow for the seeds. Look at the finished painting on the facing page for ideas on where to place the flowers along the branches.

Thirteen

GOLD HIGHLIGHTS

The soft gold highlights along the embossed, or raised, areas of the tin tile were achieved using a small pan of J.W. etc. Gold Metallic Wax and a cotton swab. Or you can also use thinned Emperor's Gold paint and a cotton swab, but the Metallic Wax gives a softer, less defined look. Don't highlight every part of every raised area—leave some parts untouched by the gold color.

Before adding the gold highlight, be sure to varnish the entire piece with at least two coats of matte polyurethane varnish.

Fourteen

FINISHING

Use the same gold paint or metallic wax to outline the center painted area with a hit-and-miss line. If your tin wall pocket does not have a hanger, use twisted wire or even twine or ribbon and attach it through two small holes drilled in the upper corners.

Cottage in Provence

To achieve that old-world look without too much effort, I chose a tile color that reminded me of the country cottages tucked away in the Provence area of southern France. Because the tile's own color was just right, no basecoating or background color was needed. ■

MATERIALS

Surface
11x12-inch (27.9cm x 30.5cm) ceramic floor tile, available at any home improvement center or tile and flooring store.

Preparation
Wipe off the tile with a soft clean cloth and transfer the pattern.

Brushes
- 1/2-inch (13mm) angle
- 5/8-inch (16mm) angle
- nos. 4 and 10 flats
- small dome brush
- 3/8-inch (10mm) angel wing
- nos. 2, 4 and 8 petal
- 10/0 striper

Additional Supplies
- Tracing paper
- Graphite paper
- Krylon 18k Gold Leafing Pen (optional)
- J.W. etc. Matte Polyurethane Varnish

Paint DecoArt Americana Acrylics

| Williamsburg Blue | Soft Black | Light Buttermilk | Burnt Sienna | Burnt Umber | Burnt Orange | Slate Grey |

| Hauser Dark Green | Hauser Med. Green | Olive Green | Red Violet | Royal Purple | Primary Red | Emperor's Gold |

Pattern

This pattern may be hand-traced or photocopied for
personal use only. Enlarge at 175% to bring up to full size.

One

Block in the door with Williamsburg Blue, the windows with Soft Black, the trim with Light Buttermilk, and the brick and terra cotta flowerpot with Burnt Sienna, using no. 4 and no. 10 flat brushes.

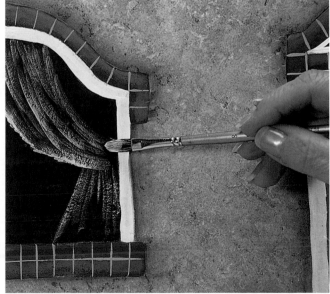

Two

Load a 5/8 inch (16mm) angle with a float of Burnt Umber and shade over the brick trim, down the sides of the doors, around the window and around the pot. Shade the brick trim itself and the pot with Burnt Umber. Highlight with a brush mix of Burnt Orange and Light Buttermilk. Paint in the path with horizontal strokes of thinned Burnt Umber.

Three

Load a 10/0 striper with Slate Grey and paint the mortar lines between the bricks in the trim above the door and over and under the window.

Four

Using a no. 8 petal brush and slightly thinned Light Buttermilk, drybrush in the sheer curtains in the window with curving strokes. Emphasize the curtain's edges with more Light Buttermilk.

Five

Load a 10/0 striper with Light Buttermilk and paint the mullions in the windows, then shade them with Slate Grey. Detail all the trim around the window, door, and eyebrow window with Slate Grey. To make the door look old, shade with vertical strokes of Soft Black, then Light Buttermilk. Let dry. Base in the antique door handle with Slate Grey and shade with Soft Black. Drybrush the diagonal light reflections in all the windows with Light Buttermilk on a small dome brush.

Six

Begin the wisteria vine and the topiary by freehanding in the branches and stems with Burnt Umber on a no. 4 petal. Load the corner of an angel wing brush with Hauser Dark Green and stipple in the first layer of foliage on the topiary ball. The second layer is Hauser Medium Green, and the lightest leaves are Olive Green. The ivy in the top of the flower pot is lined in with Hauser Dark Green; the leaves are Hauser Medium Green, Olive Green, and Light Buttermilk.

QUICK TIP

Whenever you are stippling in layers of colors to indicate areas of leaves, grass or flowers, use more color and more pressure when stippling in the first or deepest layers, and less color and less pressure for the subsequent layers. Use very little color and pressure for the topmost layer of leaves, flowers or grass.

Seven

With a no. 4 petal, stroke in the lighter leaves on the wisteria vine with Hauser Medium Green. The darker leaves are a brush mix of this same color plus Hauser Dark Green.

Eight

Double load the angel wing brush with Red Violet and Royal Purple. Lightly dab on the wisteria blossoms. Come back in with Light Buttermilk and highlight the left side of each blossom.

Nine

To paint the grassy area, load an angel wing brush with Hauser Dark Green and stipple in the first layer of grass. Let dry. The next layer is Hauser Medium Green and the lightest grass is Olive Green. Use a no. 2 petal and these same colors to pull spiky leaves along the flowerbed. With the angel wing brush, stipple in some purple flowers with Royal Purple, highlighted with Light Buttermilk.

Ten

For the flowers in the windowbox, use the corner of an angel wing brush to stipple in the greenery with Hauser Dark Green, then Hauser Medium Green and finally Olive Green. Stipple in the flowers first with Primary Red, then wet-on-wet with Light Buttermilk to highlight, using the corner of an angel wing brush.

FINISHING

The flowerbed on the right side of the path is built up with stippled layers of Hauser Dark Green, Hauser Medium Green and Olive Green for the leaves and stems, then with Primary Red and Light Buttermilk for the flowers. I added a tall purple flower in among the pink ones for more interest, using Royal Purple and Light Buttermilk.

Pull some blades of grass along the edge of the path with Hauser Dark Green and Olive Green on a 10/0 striper.

Outline the edges of the tile with either an 18k gold leafing pen, or Emperor's Gold paint and a brush. Protect your painted tile by applying a couple of coats of matte polyurethane varnish, letting dry between coats.

Three Vegetable Medley

Here is an interesting but easy way to add texture to plain tiles. These three vegetable designs are painted on top of crumpled tissue paper that has been glued to the tile, then basecoated with a warm antiqued color that is reminiscent of a Tuscan kitchen. ■

MATERIALS

Surface
8-inch (20.3cm) square ceramic tiles, available at home improvement centers and tile and flooring stores. Metal hanger available from craft supply store.

Preparation
Wipe off each tile with a soft clean cloth.

Brushes
- 1/2-inch (13mm) angle
- 5/8-inch (16mm) angle
- 3/4-inch (19mm) glazing
- nos. 2 and 12 flats
- Small and large dome
- nos. 2, 4 and 8 petal
- 1/2-inch (13mm) angel hair
- 10/0 striper
- 3/8-inch (10mm) angel mist

Additional Supplies
- J.W. etc. UnderCover (white)
- J.W. etc. Texture Gel Glaze
- White tissue wrapping paper
- Elmer's white glue
- Tracing paper
- Graphite paper
- J.W. etc. Matte Polyurethane Varnish

Paint DecoArt Americana Acrylics

Camel	Napthol Red	Cadmium Orange	Cadmium Yellow	Napa Red	Evergreen	Olive Green
Burnt Umber	Light Buttermilk	Heritage Brick	Violet Haze	Marigold	Jade Green	Yellow Green

Patterns

These patterns may be hand-traced or photocopied for
personal use only. Enlarge at 182% to bring up to full size.

Tomatoes

Bellpeppers   Carrots

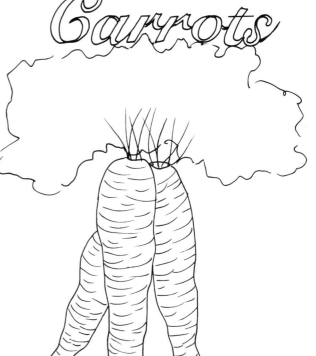

TISSUE PAPER TEXTURE

One

To give texture to plain tiles using tissue paper, start by applying a coat of J.W. etc. UnderCover in white using a 3/4-inch (19mm) glazing brush. Let this dry.

Two

Take a large piece of white tissue wrapping paper and scrunch it up into a ball. Open it up but don't smooth it out. Make a mix of two-thirds white glue and one-third water. Paint the thinned glue over the tile and onto the edges.

Three

Place the wrinkled tissue paper over the white glue. Press down with your fingers, starting in the center and working outward. Let the tissue paper extend over the edges of the tile and onto the back a little bit. Dab over the tissue paper with more glue. Do not stroke the glue on or you will pull out the wrinkles and possibly tear the paper. Let dry.

Four

Basecoat the front and edges with Camel. Let dry completely. Transfer the pattern (except for the lettering), but don't worry if the lines are not solid because of the wrinkles. After you are finished painting the tiles, you can scrape off the excess tissue paper from the back with a craft knife or sandpaper. Glue some cork or felt onto the backs of the tiles to finish them off nicely if you prefer.

Tomatoes

HIGHLIGHTS AND SHADING

One

Using a large dome brush, base in the medium value on the tomatoes with Napthol Red, a lighter value with Cadmium Orange, and a still lighter value with Cadmium Yellow. Place these values to show the roundness of the tomatoes and how they reflect light.

Two

Shade and separate the tomatoes with Napa Red on a large dome brush. Shade the indentations where the stems and calyx attach to the tops of the tomatoes.

CALYX AND STEMS

Three

Double load a no. 4 petal brush with Evergreen and Olive Green and stroke on the calyx leaves. Add the stems with a brush mix of Evergreen and Burnt Umber.

Four

Add the calyx and stem to the other tomato using the same brush and colors as in step 3. Add the final lightest highlights to the tops of the tomatoes with thinned Light Buttermilk on a 1/2-inch (13mm) angle brush. This is what makes them appear round and juicy.

FINISHING

Load a no. 8 petal brush with Burnt Umber and place a large cast shadow under the tomatoes. Deepen with Heritage Brick to warm up the cast shadow. Float a backlight of Violet Haze onto the underside edges of the tomatoes using a 1/2-inch (13mm) angle brush. Let dry.

Transfer the lettering pattern onto the tile, positioning it where you like best. Load a no. 2 flat with Evergreen and paint the lettering. Let dry.

Varnish the tile with a matte polyurethane varnish. To antique the tile, mix some Texture Gel Glaze with Burnt Umber and brush on with a 3/4-inch (19mm) glazing brush, adding more to the corners to make them darker and help frame the painted design.

QUICK TIP

Be sure to varnish your tile before applying the antiquing mixture. If you need to remove some of the antiquing or move it around, the varnish keeps the antiquing from sticking in the grooves of the tissue paper.

Bellpeppers

HIGHLIGHTS AND SHADING

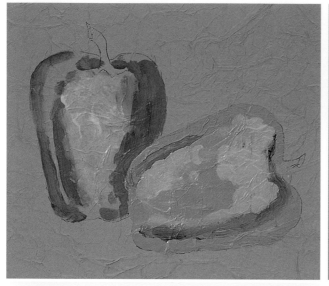

One

Using a large dome brush, block in the medium value on the yellow pepper with Marigold, the light value with Cadmium Yellow, and the darker value with Cadmium Orange. On the green pepper, the medium value is Jade Green, the light value is Olive Green, and the darker is Evergreen.

Two

On the yellow pepper, blend the three values working wet-on-wet. Re-highlight with Light Buttermilk plus a touch of Cadmium Yellow. Shade at the bottom and separate the peppers with Heritage Brick. Highlight the lightest areas with Light Buttermilk. On the green pepper, repaint and blend the three values of green. Deepen the shadows in the fold area and at the bottom with Evergreen. Re-highlight with a mix of Olive Green plus a touch of Light Buttermilk. Tint a small area with Cadmium Orange.

STEMS

Three

Base in the stems on both peppers with Jade Green. Shade them on the under-sides with Evergreen. Highlight with Light Buttermilk and backlight with Violet Haze. Tint the stem of the green pepper with Cadmium Orange.

FINISHING

Load a no. 8 petal brush with Burnt Umber and place a large cast shadow under the peppers. Deepen with Heritage Brick to warm up the cast shadow. Float a backlight of Violet Haze onto the underside edges of the peppers using a 1/2-inch (13mm) angle brush. Let dry.

Transfer the lettering pattern onto the tile, positioning it where you like best. Load a no. 2 flat with Evergreen and paint the lettering. Let dry.

Varnish the tile with a matte polyurethane varnish. To antique the tile, mix some Texture Gel Glaze with Burnt Umber and brush on, adding more to the corners to make them darker and help frame the painted design.

Carrots

HIGHLIGHTS AND SHADING

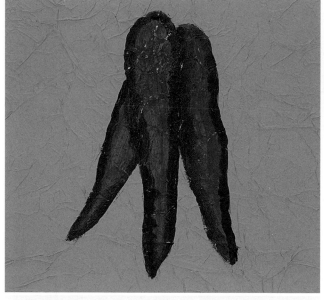

One

Using a large dome brush, block in the medium value on the carrots with Cadmium Orange. Use a small dome brush to block in the darker value of Heritage Brick along the sides of the carrots.

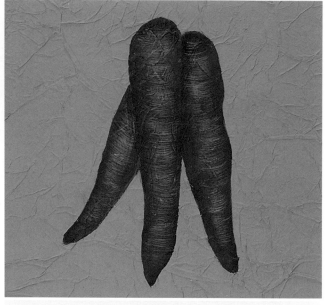

Two

Blend these two values working wet-on-wet to show the roundness of the carrots. To highlight down the centers of the carrots, load an angel hair brush with thinned Marigold and sweep little curved lines across each carrot. Repeat with thinned Cadmium Yellow. Pull lines across from the sides using Heritage Brick. Tint here and there along the edges with thinned Napthol Red. Float some thinned Evergreen onto the tops where the stems will be.

CARROT TOPS

Three

Begin the carrot tops by stroking in some stems with Evergreen on a no. 2 petal brush. Use an angel mist brush to stipple in the leaves with Evergreen first, then Jade Green, then Olive Green, and finally with Yellow Green. Stipple a little Violet Haze into the darker areas.

FINISHING

Load a no. 8 petal brush with Burnt Umber and place a large cast shadow under the carrots. Deepen with Heritage Brick to warm up the cast shadow. Float a backlight of Violet Haze onto the underside edges of the carrots using a 1/2-inch (13mm) angle brush. Let dry.

Transfer the lettering pattern onto the tile, positioning it where you like best. Load a no. 2 flat with Evergreen and paint the lettering. Let dry.

Varnish the tile with a matte polyurethane varnish. To antique the tile, mix some Texture Gel Glaze with Burnt Umber and brush on, adding more to the corners to make them darker and help frame the painted design.

Violets Tea Trivet

Make tea time special with this charming wooden trivet decorated with delicate violets. The tile in the center has a metallic coating to withstand a hot teapot, and I added glass cabinet knobs underneath to lift the trivet off the table. Almost any tea set would look lovely on this piece. ■

Surface
6-inch (15.2cm) square ceramic tile with metallic coating, available at Home Depot. Wooden frame available from The Tole Bridge.

Preparation
Sand and seal the wooden frame with J.W. etc. First Step Wood Sealer. Basecoat all of the wood with Light Buttermilk. Use a 1/2-inch (13mm) petal brush to scumble the upper left and lower right corners of the frame with Blue Chiffon, then Light Buttermilk, then Hi-Lite Flesh. Let dry. Trace and transfer the pattern.

Brushes
- 1/2-inch (13mm) angle
- 3/4-inch (19mm) glazing
- medium dome brush
- 1/2-inch (13mm) petal
- nos. 4 and 8 petal
- 10/0 striper

Additional Supplies
- J.W. etc. First Step Wood Sealer
- Sandpaper
- Tracing paper
- Graphite paper
- 4 glass cabinet knobs and screws
- J.W. etc. Matte Polyurethane Varnish

Paint DecoArt Americana Acrylics

| Light Buttermilk | Blue Chiffon | Hi-Lite Flesh | Soft Sage | Forest Green | Avocado |

| Cadmium Yellow | Plum | Winter Blue | Royal Purple | Napthol Red | Soft Sage + Forest Green + water |

Pattern

This pattern may be hand-traced or photocopied for
personal use only. Enlarge at 154% to bring up to full size.

LARGE LEAVES

One

With a 1/2-inch (13mm) petal brush, make a brush mix of Soft Sage plus Forest Green and some water. Base in the large leaves in the corners of the frame.

Two

Load a 1/2-inch (13mm) angle brush with a float of Avocado and shade each leaf at the base and along the center vein and lower half.

Three

Load a 10/0 striper with Avocado and place in the shorter vein lines on each leaf, following the outer curve of the leaf.

Four

Load a no. 8 petal brush with thinned Cadmium Yellow and tint the light areas on the leaves. Load a 1/2-inch (13mm) angle with a float of Plum and tint the edges of the leaves here and there. Let dry. Add water to the Plum and lightly add a little color and texture in and around the leaves.

QUICK TIP

Paint the leaves in as loosely as possible. This will place them in the background and complement the flowers more.

Five

Place in the transparent shadow leaves with a no. 8 petal brush and a very thinned wash of Forest Green.

Six

Double load a no. 4 petal brush with Winter Blue and Royal Purple and paint the small lavender-colored violets. For the large lavender violets, switch to a no. 8 petal brush.

Seven

For the blue violets, use the same brushes you did in step 6, but double load with Winter Blue and Plum, loading more blue than Plum.

Eight

Load a 10/0 striper with Royal Purple and shade and deepen the center of each violet with fine lines pulled out from the center onto each petal. Let dry. Paint the center of each violet with Cadmium Yellow, then add a triangle-shaped dot of Napthol Red over the Cadmium Yellow. Finish the centers with two tiny comma strokes of Light Buttermilk.

Nine

Add a calyx to each side-view violet with Forest Green. Finish off with tendrils of thinned Forest Green on a 10/0 striper. Let dry.

FINISHING

In the upper left corner, paint a smaller version of the violets-and-leaves design, using the same brushes and colors. Let dry. Paint the edge of the wooden frame with a mix of Winter Blue and Plum plus some water. When everything is dry, varnish with at least two coats of matte polyurethane varnish to protect the painting from liquids. Glue in the center trivet tile. If you don't like the metallic coated tile shown here, you can also use a plain glazed tile in a color of your choice. To lift the trivet and give it an elegant finished look, attach four glass cabinet knobs with screws to the corners on the underside of the wooden frame.

Palmmemo Board

Since this is a memo board decorated with a palm tree, I'm calling it a "Palmmemo Board" just for fun! I used black chalkboard paint to cover the memo board— you can find this paint at any home improvement or craft supply store. Hang a piece of chalk from a string attached to the board. ▪

M A T E R I A L S

Surface
10x12-inch (25.4cm x 30.5cm) ceramic floor tile available at home improvement centers. Wooden memo board from The Tole Bridge.

Preparation
If your tile feels too slippery to paint on, either spray it with Krylon Matte Finish to give it tooth, or use Etchall etching creme to remove the shine. Let dry. Trace and transfer the pattern. Paint the memo board with two coats of black chalkboard paint. The edge of the board is painted with Emperor's Gold.

Brushes
- 1/2-inch (13mm) angle
- 3/4-inch (19mm) glazing
- no. 8 flat
- 1/2-inch (13mm) angel hair
- no. 4 petal
- 10/0 striper

Additional Supplies
- Krylon Matte Finish spray or Etchall etching creme (optional)
- Masking or painter's tape
- Tracing paper
- Graphite paper
- Black, fine point permanent ink pen (optional)
- J.W. etc. Matte Polyurethane Varnish

Paint DecoArt Americana Acrylics

Fawn	Burnt Umber	Light Buttermilk	Avocado	Evergreen
Olive Green	Soft Black	Emperor's Gold	Heritage Brick	

Pattern

This pattern may be hand-traced or photocopied for personal use only. Enlarge at 120% to bring up to full size.

Palmmemo

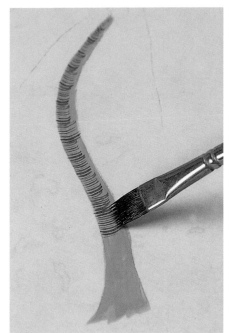

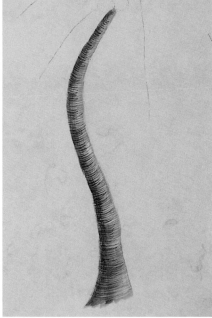

One

Base in the palm tree trunk with Fawn on a no. 8 flat. Apply two coats for good coverage. Let dry. Load a 1/2-inch (13mm) angel hair brush with Burnt Umber and pull tiny curved lines from the left side of the trunk. Let dry.

Two

Load a 1/2-inch (13mm) angel hair with Light Buttermilk thinned with water and pull tiny curved lines from the right side. Stay up on the tips of the bristles. Let dry. Corner load a 1/2-inch (13mm) angle brush with Burnt Umber and float a shade all along the left side of the trunk.

Three

Corner load a 1/2-inch (13mm) angle brush with Burnt Umber. Press and pull along the sides of the trunk where the old palm fronds were once attached and have fallen off.

Four

QUICK TIP

To blend colors and give them a soft, natural look, just dab them with your fingertips instead of using a brush or cotton swab. It's easier and faster, and you can wipe the paint off your fingers with a damp paper towel.

Load a 10/0 striper with Avocado and place in the center vein line of each palm frond branch.

Five

Load a 1/2-inch (13mm) angel hair brush with Evergreen and begin pulling leaves out from each center vein. Shorten your stroke as you get to the tip of the frond. Enrich the colors of the palm fronds by pulling more leaves with Avocado, and then a few more with Olive Green, mostly on the upper sides where the sunlight hits them.

Six

Highlight the fronds here and there with Light Buttermilk plus Olive Green, especially at the base where the fronds overlap. Tint the fronds in a few places with Emperor's Gold on an angel hair brush.

Seven

Load a no. 4 petal brush with Heritage Brick and base in the coconuts. Shade each coconut with Burnt Umber and highlight with Light Buttermilk. Paint the stems with Evergreen. Outline each coconut with Soft Black on a 10/0 striper.

Eight

Wash in the shaded grassy area under the palm tree with thinned Burnt Umber on a no. 8 flat. To paint the grasses, use a 1/2-inch (13mm) angel hair brush and start with Evergreen. Stay up on the very tips of the bristles. Add some lighter grass with Avocado, then switch to a 10/0 striper and Olive Green for the lightest grasses. Base in the gold shield with Emperor's Gold on a no. 8 flat. Let dry. With a 1/2-inch (13mm) angle brush, float a shade of Heritage Brick around the outside edge of the shield to give it some curvature. Don't shade the gold dots.

Nine

While the gold shield is drying, thin some Burnt Umber with water and dab on shading around the palm tree trunk and fronds. Pat the shading with your fingers to soften.

Ten

Outline the gold shield and add the crosshatch lines using either a black permanent ink pen, or Soft Black paint on a 10/0 striper. Use either for the lettering as well. Outline the first letter "P" with Emperor's Gold.

FINISHING

To give your palm tree tile a nice finished look, frame it with a wide black border edged along the inside with gold. Tape off the edges with masking tape or painter's tape, leaving about a 1/2-inch (13mm) wide band. Paint this black. Remove the tape and let dry. Use a 10/0 striper and Emperor's Gold to paint a gold outline next to the black band.

    The frame that holds the tile in place on the memo board is painted with Light Buttermilk. Sponge on a little Fawn to antique it if you want.

    Varnish the tile, the framed edge, and the gold edge with a matte polyurethane varnish. Don't varnish the black chalkboard paint or it will no longer accept the chalk.

Perfume and Roses

Place a few fingertip towels and your favorite perfume bottles in this little cabinet and add a touch of old-fashioned romance to your dressing table or powder room. The roses are easy to paint on this small ceramic tile and the gold lettering gives it an elegant effect. ■

MATERIALS

Surface
5x8-inch (12.7cm x 20.3cm) ceramic tile from any home improvement center or tile and flooring store. Cabinet from The Tole Bridge.

Preparation
Lightly spray the tile with matte spray sealer. Trace and transfer the pattern, except for the lettering.

Brushes
- 1/2-inch (13mm) angle
- 3/4-inch (19mm) glazing
- 3/8-inch (10mm) angel wing
- nos. 2, 4 and 8 petal
- 10/0 striper

Additional Supplies
- DecoArt Matte Spray Sealer
- Krylon 18k Gold Leafing Pen
- Tracing paper
- Graphite paper
- DecoArt Weathered Wood Crackling Medium
- Clear glass knob for cabinet drawer

Paint DecoArt Americana Acrylics

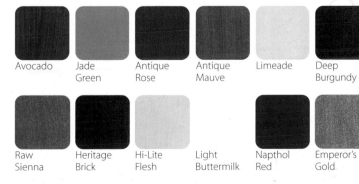

Avocado	Jade Green	Antique Rose	Antique Mauve	Limeade	Deep Burgundy	Evergreen

Raw Sienna	Heritage Brick	Hi-Lite Flesh	Light Buttermilk	Napthol Red	Emperor's Gold	Red Violet

Pattern

This pattern may be hand-traced or photocopied for personal use only. Enlarge at 120% to bring up to full size.

V I N E S ,   L E A V E S   A N D   R O S E S

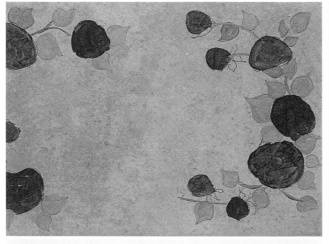

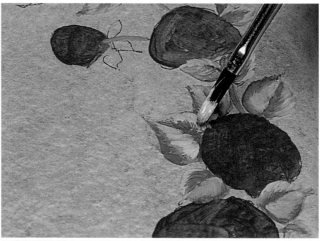

One

Paint in the vines with Avocado tipped with Jade Green on a 10/0 striper. Load a no. 4 petal brush with the same colors and a little water and base in all of the leaves. Base in the peach-colored roses with Antique Rose. Base in the pink roses and rosebuds with Antique Mauve.

Two

Drybrush a little Limeade into the lighter areas of the leaves, and Avocado into the darker areas.

Three

Using a 1/2-inch (13mm) angle brush and Deep Burgundy, float a tint on the edges of the leaves.

Four

Load a 10/0 striper with Evergreen and place in vein lines on the leaves, pulling them outward from the center vein line.

Five

Using the corner of a 3/8-inch (10mm) angel wing brush, stipple in background greens with Avocado. Touch with your finger to soften and blend a little.

Six

With a no. 2 petal brush, place in a few transparent background leaves with thinned Raw Sienna. Pull stems into them with Avocado on a 10/0 striper.

Seven

Use a no. 4 petal brush with Heritage Brick to paint in the center cup and the shaded side of the peach rose and rosebud.

Eight

Place highlights on the peach rose and rosebud with Hi-Lite Flesh, making curving strokes that follow the shape of the rose.

Nine

Re-establish the shaded areas of the peach rose and rosebud with a brush mix of Antique Rose and Heritage Brick.

Ten

Paint in some individual petals around the cup of the rose and rosebud with Hi-Lite Flesh.

Eleven

On the pink rose and rosebuds, deepen the shaded sides and the cup with Deep Burgundy.

QUICK TIP

Use the chisel edge as well as the flat edge of your brush, and stay back on your brush handle to lightly pull the highlights and shadows on the roses, overlapping the colors as you go.

Twelve

Add lighter petals to the pink roses with short strokes of Light Buttermilk on a no. 4 petal brush. Tint the area between the shaded and highlighted sides of the pink roses with Napthol Red.

Thirteen

Paint the lightest petals on the pink roses and rosebuds with Light Buttermilk. Dot in seeds with Emperor's Gold. Tint with a little Red Violet. Load a 10/0 striper with Evergreen and paint the calyxes on the rosebuds and some soft tendrils.

FINISHING

Transfer the lettering pattern to the tile, then paint the lettering, the swash and crosshatching with Emperor's Gold. Shade the left side of each letter hit-or-miss with Heritage Brick. Outline the edge of the tile with an 18k gold leafing pen. Let dry. Protect the finished tile with a matte spray varnish.

The wooden cabinet the tile is set into has a crackled finish. Using a 3/4-inch (19mm) glazing brush, basecoat the entire cabinet with Emperor's Gold. This is the color that shows through the crackles. Next, paint on a heavy coat of DecoArt Weathered Wood Crackling Medium, following the manufacturer's instructions. Let dry, and paint over the Weathered Wood with a heavy coat of Light Buttermilk. Let dry.

French Country Rooster

A plump and colorful rooster is painted here with loose, almost impressionistic strokes. The large tile with rounded corners makes an attractive backsplash behind a sink or cooktop, and brings a touch of French country style to your kitchen decor. ■

Paint DecoArt Americana Acrylics

Payne's Grey • Ultramarine Blue • Cerulean Blue • Dioxazine Purple • Violet Haze • Viridian Green • Cadmium Orange • Burnt Sienna

Deep Burgundy • Raw Sienna • Camel • Cadmium Yellow • Light Buttermilk • Burnt Umber • Avocado

Pattern

This pattern may be hand-traced or photocopied for personal use only. Enlarge at 154% to bring up to full size.

BREAST AND TAIL FEATHERS

One

Begin painting the rooster's breast feathers with Payne's Grey on a 1/2-inch (13mm) petal brush. Pull your strokes downward in the direction of feather growth.

Two

Gradually add Ultramarine Blue, still stroking in the direction of feather growth. Repeat with Cerulean Blue, then with Dioxazine Purple. Don't rinse your brush between colors; just wipe it on a paper towel when the paint builds up.

Three

Now move to the tail feathers and repeat steps 1 and 2 with the same brush and colors, stroking in a high arch and tapering off toward the end. Fill in with lots of feathers.

Four

While the paint is still wet, stroke in a few feathers of Violet Haze. If you think you have put in too many lighter value feathers, go back in while the paint is still wet with your base color (Payne's Grey) and darken the tail feathers a bit.

QUICK TIP

Be sure to use the chisel edge and the flat edge of the brush to create the feathers. This will give you a variation in size and shape and allows you to paint quickly wet-on-wet. Don't worry if your feathers extend beyond the pattern lines. This is a loosely painted rooster with a slightly exaggerated body size.

BREAST AND TAIL FEATHERS

Five

In the breast area, stroke in a few feathers of Violet Haze, then Viridian Green, on the lighter, outside areas of the breast and front of the legs. The green does not muddy the violet; it just lightens it a bit.

Six

Finish layering the tail feathers with a few strokes of Viridian Green. Let dry. Finally, stroke in just a very few feathers of Cadmium Orange.

BACK WING FEATHERS

Seven

Moving on to the wing feathers, base in the first layer of feathers with Burnt Sienna on a no. 2 petal brush, stroking in the downward direction of feather growth.

Eight

While the paint is still wet, stroke in the next layers of feathers with Cerulean Blue, then with Deep Burgundy.

Nine

Highlight a few of the back wing feathers with Violet Haze, then with a little bit of Cadmium Orange here and there. Let dry.

Ten

Load a 1/2-inch (13mm) petal brush with Raw Sienna and base in the first layer of head, neck and side feathers. You may need two coats for good coverage.

Eleven

Begin the next layer of feathers by stroking in Camel, then Cadmium Yellow, following the downward direction of feather growth. Overlap the back wing feathers a little bit.

Twelve

The next layer of feathers is a brush mix of Cadmium Yellow and Light Buttermilk. Tint here and there with a little Cadmium Orange.

Thirteen

Add some backlights with Violet Haze in the feathers under the wattle to show shading and along the lower edges to show where the feathers curve inward toward the body.

Fourteen

Double load a no. 8 petal brush with Cadmium Orange and Deep Burgundy and base in the rooster's comb and wattle, using a patting motion with your brush. To highlight, scumble in a mix of Cadmium Orange and Light Buttermilk. Shade with a touch of Violet Haze.

Fifteen

Load a no. 2 petal brush with Payne's Grey and base in the eye and the opening of the beak. Let dry. Base the beak with a brush mix of Camel and a touch of Cadmium Yellow. Shade the beak while it is wet with Burnt Sienna, and highlight with little dashes of Light Buttermilk. Outline the top of the beak with Burnt Sienna and dot in the nostril with Payne's Grey. Add the reflective highlight in the eye with Light Buttermilk.

LEGS AND FEET

Sixteen

Base in the legs and feet with a brush mix of Camel and Cadmium Yellow. Highlight one side of the legs and feet with Cadmium Yellow. Shade the other side with Burnt Sienna. Pull a few small feathers down over the tops of the legs with Payne's Grey on a 10/0 striper.

Seventeen

Wash in the ground underneath the rooster with Burnt Umber on the shadow side and a mix of Camel and Burnt Umber on the light side. Let dry. Pull some blades of grass with Avocado and a little Burnt Umber on a 10/0 striper. Enrich the highlights on the lower belly and leg feathers with a drybrush of Light Buttermilk.

ANTIQUING

Eighteen

To antique the edges of the tile, use a damp natural sea sponge and dab on some Burnt Umber, concentrating more in the four corners than along the edges. Flip the sponge over to a clean side and mottle the Burnt Umber to soften and blend it out towards the center.

FINISHING

After all the paint and antiquing is dry, trim the outer edge of the tile on all four sides with a border of Avocado on a no. 12 flat brush. I did this freehand to maintain the loose impressionistic look of the tile's design, but if you prefer you can use masking or painters tape to help give you a straight line. Two coats may be needed for complete coverage. Let dry.

Use a 3/4-inch (19mm) glazing brush and protect your painted tile with at least two coats of matte polyurethane varnish, letting dry between coats. If you are using this tile as a backsplash, several coats of varnish are recommended.

Hydrangeas & Bird's Nest

Surface
12-inch (30.5cm) square ceramic tile from any home improvement center or tile and flooring store. Choose a color that is soft and warm to harmonize with the colors of the design.

Preparation
If your tile has a shiny surface, lightly spray the tile with matte spray sealer. Trace and transfer the major outlines of the pattern, not the details.

Brushes
- 1/2-inch (13mm) angle
- nos. 2, 4 and 8 petal
- 10/0 striper

Additional Supplies
- DecoArt Matte Spray Sealer
- Tracing paper
- Graphite paper
- J.W. etc. Gloss Polyurethane Varnish

Here is a glimpse of nature at its most touching—with newly blossoming hydrangeas cradling a little bird's nest of blue eggs. The gentle colors in this design are fresh and springlike against the soft background of the tile's natural color. ■

Paint DecoArt Americana Acrylics

Burnt Umber

Hi-Lite Flesh

Moon Yellow

Uniform Blue

Hauser Med. Green

Olive Green

Green Mist

Deep Burgundy

Light Buttermilk

Hauser Medium Green + Burnt Umber + a touch of Olive Green

Eight

To begin the white hydrangeas, scumble in a heavy amount of Hauser Medium Green and Olive Green using a no. 8 petal brush. Add a touch of Burnt Umber here and there.

Nine

While the scumble is still wet, stroke in the petals of the florets with Light Buttermilk, picking up the scumble colors as you go. Pick up more Light Buttermilk on your brush for each floret.

Ten

To add warmth and color variations to the white hydrangeas, pick up Hi-Lite Flesh once in a while instead of Light Buttermilk to paint the florets.

Eleven

Begin the pink hydrangeas by scumbling in a heavy amount of Deep Burgundy. Add a touch of Burnt Umber here and there.

Twelve

While the scumble color is still wet, load a no. 8 petal brush with Hi-Lite Flesh and stroke in the petals of the florets, picking up the Deep Burgundy as you go. Keep reloading your brush with Hi-Lite Flesh for each new floret. Do not rinse your brush, just wipe excess paint on a paper towel. Let dry.

QUICK TIP

The secret to painting hydrangeas is to keep picking up fresh color on your brush every time you paint a new floret. This separates the petals and keeps the edges distinct.

Thirteen

Dot in the oval centers of each floret with Moon Yellow on a no. 2 petal brush. Shade the centers with a tiny line of Deep Burgundy on a 10/0 striper. Let dry.

FINISHING

Lightly spray your tile with matte spray sealer to lock down the colors. Corner load a 1/2-inch (13mm) angle brush into Deep Burgundy and shade the bottom portions of the pink hydrangeas to give roundness and form to the blossoms. To separate the white hydrangeas, shade between them with Olive Green. Shade the bottom portions of the white hydrangeas with Olive Green to give them roundness. Re-highlight some of the petals at the tops of the blossoms if needed, but don't use too much paint or you will cover up the variegated petals already there. Once all the paint is dry, protect the tile with a gloss polyurethane varnish.

Old World Winery

Tiles with scenes painted on them are an easy and colorful way to add warmth and charm to your home. Scenic tiles are often used as a backsplash behind cooktops and sinks. This six-tile scenic tray would look wonderful on a kitchen island or as a serving or display piece in a wine cellar or wet bar. ■

MATERIALS

Surface
Six 6-inch (15.2cm) square white ceramic tiles from any home improvement center. Wooden tray from Ceramics and Crafts Warehouse.

Preparation
If your tiles have a shiny glaze, deglaze them with Etchall etching creme, following the manufacturer's instructions.

Brushes
- no. 10 flat
- 3/4-inch (19mm) glazing
- 5/8-inch (16mm) angle
- 1/2-inch (13mm) angle
- nos. 2 and 4 petal
- 1/2-inch (13mm) angel hair
- 1/2-inch (13mm) petal
- 3/8-inch (10mm) angel wing
- Fingertip brush
- 10/0 striper

Additional Supplies
- Tracing paper
- Graphite paper
- Blue painter's tape
- Premixed white tile grout
- J.W. etc. Matte Polyurethane Varnish

Paint DecoArt Americana Acrylics

Blue Chiffon | Uniform Blue | Light Buttermilk | Sapphire | Red Violet | Violet Haze | Jade Green | Avocado | Viridian Green

Golden Straw | Burnt Umber | Evergreen | Olive Green | Titanium White | Antique Rose | Soft Black | Raw Sienna

Pattern

This pattern may be hand-traced or photocopied for
personal use only. Enlarge at 185% to bring up to full size.

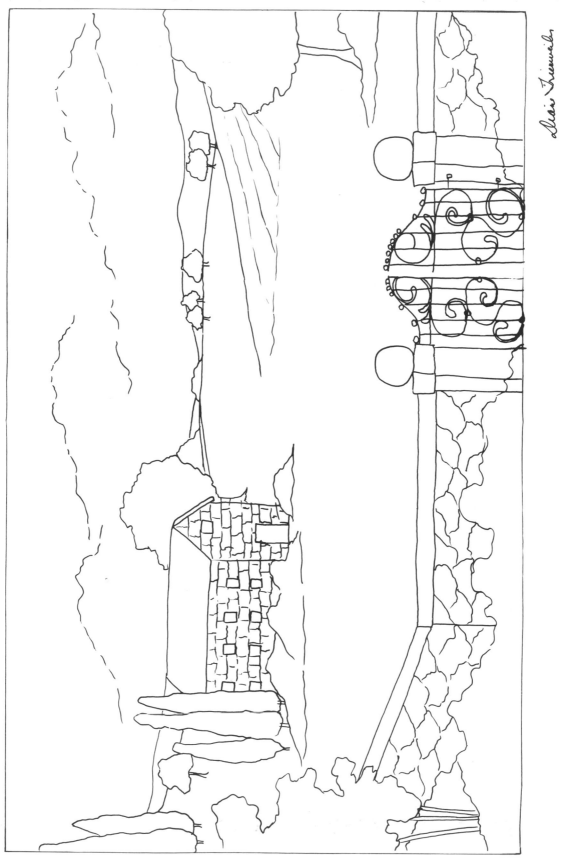

One

Arrange your six tiles as shown in the tray, but do not grout them in yet. Secure them with 1-inch (25mm) wide blue painter's tape around the outside edge, making a border. This border will be painted later after the vineyard scene is completed. Once the tiles are in place, trace and transfer the pattern. Transfer only the major outlines, not all the details. The wrought iron gate pattern will be transferred later.

If you intend to use these tiles in a backsplash on a kitchen wall, tape them to a flat board rather than a tray, paint the scene, varnish them, and then grout them onto the wall.

Two

Using a 1/2-inch (13mm) petal brush, make a brush mix of Blue Chiffon and Uniform Blue. Scumble in the sky area, keeping the darker blue toward the top and the lighter blue toward the horizon. Deglazed tiles will soak up the paint so put on a generous amount. Add a little water to your brush as you proceed.

Three

Load a fingertip brush with Light Buttermilk and place in the clouds. Stay back on your brush handle and leave the bristles sitting on the surface. Make small circular motions for fluffy clouds.

Four

Dampen a 5/8-inch (16mm) angle brush and load the toe (the longest part of the bristles) into Sapphire. Float this color along the top edge of the sky to deepen the color. Blend out into the lighter sky color below so there is no distinct line of demarcation.

Five

Using a 1/2-inch (13mm) petal brush, tint the sky in a hit-and-miss fashion with Red Violet that has been thinned with a lot of water. This is a very strong color so be sure to keep it subtle. You are just trying to enrich the color of the sky, not change it.

Six

The hills in the far distance are painted in with a brush mix of Violet Haze, Light Buttermilk and a little water. Use a 1/2-inch (13mm) petal brush, sweeping the colors in horizontally.

Seven

Wash over the distant hills with very thinned Sapphire to cool them and set them into the background. Base in the middle-ground and foreground fields with a brush mix of Jade Green and Light Buttermilk on a 1/2-inch (13mm) petal brush. Keep your strokes horizontal, following the low hills and valleys.

Eight

Dampen a 5/8-inch (16mm) angle brush and load the toe into Avocado. Float this along the edges of the fields to separate the hills and slopes of the valley. Use this same color to shade under the winery building, in the lower grassy areas, and along the path.

Nine

Tint the grassy fields here and there with touches of Viridian Green thinned with water. Load a 3/8-inch (10mm) angel wing brush with Golden Straw and stipple in some dry grasses in the middle field. Sweep some of this color into the other grassy fields as well. If the color becomes too yellow, just sweep some thinned Avocado over the area to soften the color.

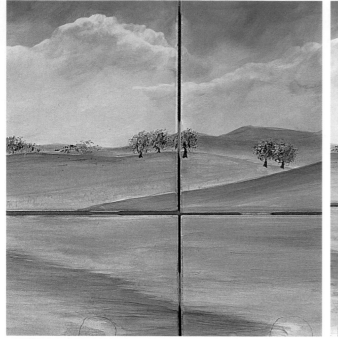

Ten

Load a 10/0 striper with Burnt Umber and paint the tree trunks for the trees on the distant hill. Stipple in the tree foliage using Evergreen, then Olive Green, on the corner of a 3/8-inch (10mm) angel wing brush. Highlight on the sunlit side with just a touch of Golden Straw.

Eleven

Double load the angel wing brush with Red Violet and Titanium White. Stipple in rows of lavender in the far right field.

Twelve

To paint the large tree in front of the lavender field, place in the trunk with Burnt Umber, and highlight with Light Buttermilk. Stipple in the first (darkest) layer of leaves with Evergreen, the next layer with Avocado, then Olive Green, then Olive Green plus Titanium White for the lighter leaves. Stipple on a little Golden Straw for the final highlight on the sunlit side.

Thirteen

Stipple in grasses in the shaded area underneath the tree with Evergreen and Olive Green. Stipple in flowers with Antique Rose, Red Violet and Sapphire. Tint the tree foliage with a little thinned Viridian Green, Antique Rose and Violet Haze.

Fourteen

Base in the walls of the winery building using Light Buttermilk, and the roof with Antique Rose. Load a no. 2 petal brush with thinned Soft Black and base in the windows and door. Shade the left sides with a float of Soft Black. Outline the roof edges with Soft Black. Paint the mortar lines of the winery walls free-hand with Raw Sienna on a 10/0 striper. The tree behind the winery is painted the same way as in step 10. The shrubs in the far distance behind the tree are stippled in with Antique Rose.

Fifteen

Corner load a 1/2-inch (13mm) angle brush and shade the walls of the winery with a float of Burnt Umber, then with a float of Soft Black, along the corner and under the eaves. Tint the walls with thinned Golden Straw to give a feeling of sunshine and warmth.

Sixteen

Shade the left side of the roof with Antique Rose and a little Soft Black on a 1/2-inch (13mm) angel hair brush. Highlight the right side of the roof with with a mix of Antique Rose and Light Buttermilk. Tint with Golden Straw. Backlight the shaded part of the roof with Red Violet. Add a line of Light Buttermilk along the roof ridge and gable end to highlight.

Seventeen

The tall, columnar cypress trees to the left of the winery are painted with the same colors as the deciduous trees. Because they are so tall and narrow, use a no. 4 petal brush to stipple in Evergreen first for the darkest leaves, then Avocado, then Olive Green. The lighter leaves are Olive Green and Titanium White, and the highlight on the sunlit side is Golden Straw. Tint with Viridian Green here and there. Add a backlight of Violet Haze to the darkest side of the trees. The shrubbery in front of the winery is stippled in with Evergreen, then Olive Green, and the flowers are stipples of Sapphire, Golden Straw and Red Violet. The trunks are Burnt Umber.

Eighteen

The old stone wall at the gated entrance to the winery is painted in a warm tone that picks up the colors of the building. Load a no. 10 flat with Light Buttermilk and Raw Sienna and scumble in the front of the wall. Leave the colors mottled looking, don't blend them too much.

Nineteen

Paint in the top of the wall, the stone posts and the decorative ball finials with Light Buttermilk. Load a 10/0 striper with Raw Sienna and freehand in the curved mortar lines between the stones on the front of the wall.

SHADING AND HIGHLIGHTS

Twenty

Use a 5/8-inch (16mm) angle brush and a mix of Raw Sienna and Burnt Umber to shade the walls and form the corners. Switch to a 1/2-inch (13mm) angle to shade the posts and ball finials at the gate openings.

Twenty-One

Highlight the sides of the ball finials and the tops of the walls with Titanium White. Shade the corners of the walls at the gate opening with thinned Soft Black. Tint the wall with thinned Antique Rose, then backlight with Violet Haze in the shaded areas.

FLOWERING TREE AND BUSHES

Twenty-Two

Paint the trunk and branches of the flowering tree on the left with Burnt Umber, then highlight with Light Buttermilk. Use an angel wing brush to stipple in the tree's foliage, starting with Burnt Umber, the Red Violet, then Red Violet plus Light Buttermilk. Begin stippling in the foliage of the bushes in front of the wall with Evergreen. Highlight with stipples of Olive Green.

FLOWERING SHRUBS

Twenty-Three

Using an angel hair brush, begin stippling in the flowers in front of the stone wall with Golden Straw. Then stipple in a bit fewer flowers with Antique Rose, then even fewer flowers with Sapphire, and finally very few with Red Violet. Keeping the blue painters tape on while you stipple makes it easier to do—you can be freer with the brush and it doesn't matter how much paint gets on the tape.

WROUGHT IRON GATE

Twenty-Four

Transfer the gate pattern onto your tiles. Load a 10/0 striper with Soft Black and paint in the lines of the wrought iron gate. Highlight the gate here and there with Light Buttermilk on a 10/0 striper.

FINISHING

Remove the blue painter's tape from all four sides of the design. Base in the border with Light Buttermilk. Let all the paint dry completely, then apply matte polyurethane varnish to the tiles to protect them. Let dry and apply another coat of varnish.

To grout the tiles into the tray, take the tiles out of the tray and cover the bottom of the wooden tray with premixed white tile grout, using a putty knife. Spread the grout evenly. Place the tiles back into the tray and fill in between the tiles and around the edges with more grout. Make sure your tiles are aligned the way they were when you painted them. Immediately wipe off the tiles with a damp rag to remove any grouting from the painted areas. Use a very soft rag and do not rub too hard or you might remove the paint. Wipe off any residue from the wooden tray as well.

If you want to use your tray to serve drinks, you may want to place a piece of clear Plexiglas over the tiles to protect them from spills and stains.

Resources

U.S. Retailers

Ceramic floor and wall tiles:
Available in many sizes, shapes and colors at home improvement centers such as Lowe's and Home Depot.

DecoArt Americana Acrylic Paints:
- **DecoArt**
  P.O. Box 386
  Stanford, KY 40484
  1-800-367-3047
  www.decoart.com

Sealers, Mediums, and Varnishes:
- **J.W. etc.**
  11972 Hertz St.
  Moorpark, CA 93021
  805-529-9500
  www.jwetc.com

Delta Ceramcoat Two-Step Fine Crackle Finish:
- **Delta Technical Coatings, Inc.**
  2550 Pellissier Pl.
  Whittier, CA 90601
  1-800-423-4135
  www.deltacrafts.com

Brushes:
- **Loew-Cornell**
  563 Chestnut Ave.
  Teaneck, NJ 07666-2490
  201-836-7070
  www.loew-cornell.com

Matte Finish Spray; 18k Gold Leafing Pen:
- **Krylon**
  1-800-4KRYLON
  www.krylon.com

Metal Stands and Easels:
- **Elegance in Easels**
  2206 N. Country Club Road
  Tucson, AZ 85716-2832
  800-325-8286
  www.easels.com

Tiles, Trivets, Trays, etc.:
- **Ceramics and Crafts Warehouse**
  13595 12th St.
  Chino, CA 91710
  909-627-4139

Diane Trierweiler's Signature Brushes:
- **The Tole Bridge**
  1875 Norco Drive
  Norco, CA 92860
  951-272-6918
  e-mail: Tolebridge@aol.com

Tin Tile Wall Pocket:
- **Painters Paradise Jo C. & Co.**
  C-10, 950 Ridge Rd.
  Claymont, DE 19703-3553
  302-798-3897
  www.paintersparadise.com

Tin Ceiling Tiles:
- **Viking Woodcrafts, Inc.**
  1317 8th St. SE
  Waseca, MN 56093
  800-328-0116
  www.vikingwoodcrafts.com

Etchall etching creme; etchall dip 'n etch:
- **B & B Etching Products, Inc.**
  19721 N. 98th Ave.
  Peoria, AZ 85382
  888-382-4255
  www.etchall.com

Canadian Retailers
- **Crafts Canada**
  www.craftscanada.ca

- **Folk Art Enterprises**
  P.O. Box 1088
  Ridgetown, ON, N0P 2C0
  Tel: 800-265-9434
  www.folkartenterprises.com

- **MacPherson Arts & Crafts**
  91 Queen St. E.
  P.O. Box 1810
  St. Mary's, ON, N4X 1C2
  Tel: 800-238-6663
  www.macphersoncrafts.com

- **Maureen McNaughton Enterprises**
  RR #2
  Belwood, Ontario, N0B 1J0
  Tel: 519-843-5648
  www.maureenmcnaughton.com

- **Mercury Art & Craft Supershop**
  332 Wellington Rd.
  London, ON, N6C 4P7
  Tel: 519-434-1636

- **Town & Country Folk Art Supplies**
  93 Green Lane
  Thornhill, ON, L3T 6K6
  Tel: 905-882-0199

U.K. Retailers
- **Atlantis Art Materials**
  7-9 Plumber's Row
  London E1 1EQ
  020 7377 8855
  www.atlantisart.co.uk

- **Crafts World (head office)**
  No. 8 North Street
  Guildford
  Surrey GU1 4 AF
  07000 757070

- **Green & Stone**
  259 King's Road
  London SW3 5EL
  020 7352 6521

- **Hobby Crafts (head office)**
  River Court
  Southern Sector
  Bournemouth International Airport
  Christchurch
  Dorset BH23 6SE
  0800 272387

Index

N The best in home decorating instruction is from **North Light Books**!

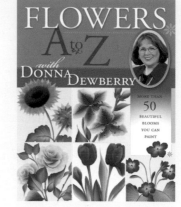

Flowers A to Z with Donna Dewberry

Painting your favorite flowers is easy and fun with Donna Dewberry's popular one-stroke technique! You'll see how to paint more than 50 garden flowers and wildflowers in an array of stunning colors. Discover Donna's secrets for painting leaves, vines, foliage, flower petals, blossoms, and floral bouquets. Add beauty and elegance to any project including furniture, walls, pottery, birdbaths and more!

ISBN 1-58180-484-9, paperback, 144 pages, #32803-K

Painted Illusions
Create Stunning Trompe L'oeil Effects with Stencils

Add incredible beauty and elegance to your home with *Painted Illusions*. Even if you've never painted before, you can achieve professional-quality results with these simple stencil techniques and Melanie Royals' easy-to-follow direction. In 19 step-by-step projects, you'll learn to create beautiful wall finishes that mimic fabrics such as linen, silk and damask as well as trompe l'oeil effects such as leather, porcelain, oak paneling, granite, carved stone, and more.

ISBN 1-58180-548-9, paperback, 128 pages, # 32899-K

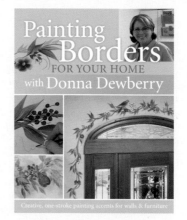

Painting Borders for Your Home with Donna Dewberry

America's favorite decorative painter shows you how to use her popular one-stroke painting method to create colorful borders that give character and style to any home. Jam-packed with borders for every room in your home, from the laundry room to the foyer, from the dining room to the master bath, these easy-to-paint borders range from whimsical to sophisticated and everything in-between. See how adding a simple border to a wall or furniture can transform an ordinary room into a masterpiece!

ISBN 1-58180-600-0, paperback, 128 pages, #33125-K

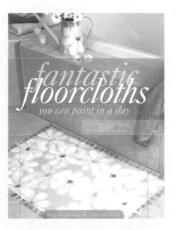

Fantastic Floorcloths You Can Paint in a Day

Refresh your home decor with these inexpensive and fun-to-paint canvas floorcloths. You'll find 25 colorful and up-to-date designs you can paint in a few hours using durable acrylic paints, plus 12 bonus accessory ideas for a coordinated look. Includes floorcloth designs for every room in the house, every season of the year, for beginners and experienced painters alike. Decorate your home today with pretty florals, colorful graphics, holiday motifs, and cute and colorful designs for kids' rooms.

ISBN 1-58180-603-5, paperback, 128 pages, #33161-K

These books and other fine North Light titles are available at your local arts & crafts retailer, bookstore, online supplier or by calling 1-800-448-0915 in North America or 0870 2200220 in the United Kingdom.